THE
BATTLE FOR BERLIN
ONTARIO

An Historical Drama

W.R. Chadwick

Wilfrid Laurier University Press

Canadian Cataloguing in Publication Data

Chadwick, W. R. (William Rowley), 1934-
The battle for Berlin, Ontario

Includes bibliographical references and index.
ISBN 0-88920-226-5

1. Kitchener (Ontario) – Name.   2. Kitchener (Ontario) –
History – 20th century.   3. World War, 1914-1918 –
Ontario – Kitchener – Influence.   I. Title.

FC3099.K58C48 1992   971.3'45   C92-095189-9
F1059.5.K58C48 1992

Copyright © 1992

Wilfrid Laurier University Press
Waterloo, Ontario, Canada
N2L 3C5

Cover design by Connolly Design Inc.

Cover photograph: Soldiers on King St.
Inside front flap: Sergeant Major Granville Blood
(Both photographs courtesy of the Schneider Corporation Archives,
Norman Schneider Collection)

Printed in Canada

The Battle for Berlin, Ontario: An Historical Drama has been produced from
a manuscript supplied in electronic form by the author.

Contents

Foreword

For many Canadians, World War I (1914-18) marked the end of an era. Nostalgic memories of life as it might have been before the war were popularized by Canada's favourite humorist, Stephen Leacock, in *Sunshine Sketches of a Little Town*, his delightful stories of the fictional Ontario town of Mariposa. Leacock, in fact, travelled throughout southern Ontario during the war years giving a series of readings of these very stories in an effort to raise money for the war. Many residents of Berlin, Ontario, may well have been in the audience eagerly listening to his humorous and warmhearted depictions of an idyllic small town in Ontario, portraying an innocence that was being lost even as he spoke. Curiously, many of us have never really doubted the reality of Leacock's fictional *Sunshine Sketches*. For the residents of Berlin, Ontario, it was clear that Berlin was not Mariposa, nor were the events taking place in their city fictional, although today many might doubt that the happenings described in William Chadwick's history could actually have taken place in Ontario.

These were traumatic times for many of Berlin's citizens and in this city's history. Not only would the historic name, Berlin, be replaced by that of Britain's most famous warrior, Field Marshall Lord Kitchener, but there would also be soldiers with fixed bayonets on the city's streets. Clearly, this was not the fictional Mariposa. Nor is this story fictional. Sergeant Major Granville Blood might well have been a character invented by Leacock, but in fact he was, if anything, "larger than life." Press gangs led by soldiers forcing young men to enlist for military service were perhaps common on the streets of Toronto, but they were also here. A Lutheran minister, dragged from his home and family, bloodied on the streets and forcibly detained by an unruly mob of soldiers, threatened with dire consequences for failing to leave the country, could not have existed except in fiction. Yet, those events did happen here, on the streets of Berlin during the years of World War I. How could this have been and why has it taken so long for Canadians to come to terms with the reality of their own past?

William Chadwick's story of life in this small Ontario city during the "Great War" describes not just the ethnic tensions in a city whose background was primarily Germanic, but also the social problems which resulted when as many as 500 or 600 young soldiers were housed in barracks or billeted throughout the town, anxious to fight in an overseas war, but finding themselves confined to route marches to nearby villages or to calisthenics in Victoria Park. That they did so is not surprising; what is of interest, however, is the reaction of the city's municipal leaders and the attempts by politicians and other civic leaders to exploit this tension for their own advantage. The "Great Name Change Debate" which occurred in Berlin in 1916 is a dramatic illustration of the way that politics can be used for personal interests and conflicting purposes. So fundamental an event in the life of a city has profoundly affected Berlin/Kitchener to the present day, yet it is the power of Chadwick's prose that he describes these events as if they happened only yesterday.

This book tells how and why this community was riven by wartime tensions, and in doing so it has provided a lost chapter in the life of Kitchener and its people. Chadwick tells his story with a dramatic flair; yet his research is painstakingly accurate, and he allows many of the characters in this drama to speak in their own words. We owe a debt to William Chadwick for recovering this lost history and for bringing it to life in such an entertaining and compelling manner. From this book we can learn much about our community and about relations within that community as we plan for its future.

Waterloo, Ontario   Kenneth McLaughlin
September 1992

Preface

When I first began researching the Berlin name change it was with the intention of turning this fascinating piece of Ontario history into a play, but after a time I decided that what was needed first was a reasonably detailed account of what actually occurred in Berlin in 1916, and that the proper form for this was a more conventional chronicle of events. The play could come later.

The general outlines of these events are, of course, well known — though there still seems to be some confusion about some of the incidents; what I have here tried to add is the shading. Not simply what happened, but how it happened and why it happened, and, perhaps most important of all, who made it happen.

What follows, then, is the week-by-week, and sometimes day-by-day, story of a traumatic affair that is still capable of generating a remarkable degree of emotion in this Ontario city. The account is based on newspaper reports, military records, diaries, conversations with those who were living at the time, and so on. It hardly needs adding that, like any good historian, I interpret these reports and records in my own way; and, indeed, it will soon become clear to the reader that I "take sides," which adds a flavour of drama to my account and may well provoke the reader.

It is also conceivable that someone might object that my opinion is coloured by a specifically 1990s perspective in that I attack the cheap emotionalism, the demagoguery, the jingoism, the propaganda of the time. However, many of those who lived through those difficult years were equally appalled at these manifestations of human idiocy. I refer here not simply to the Bernard Shaws and the Mrs. Pankhursts of the wider scene but, more importantly for this study, to the average citizens of Berlin, Ontario, who found themselves at the centre of an emotional war of words, and sometimes worse. Indeed, an appropriate dedication of this book would be to those Berliners, and they were very much a silent majority as these pages will argue, who had the name of their city unfairly taken from them.

One important point needs to be made about the military unrest in Berlin. This city was not by any means the only one in the country that had to put up with turbulent soldiers. There are many accounts of broken windows, donnybrooks in beer parlours, and so on, in towns throughout the Dominion where troops were billeted. In Toronto, to take one small example from the time which I am writing about, an elaborate temperance rally was comprehensively disrupted by local recruits, and several university students had to seek medical assistance. The difference in Berlin was that here this behaviour was fiercer, lasted longer, and, most important of all, was more organized and focussed – for reasons that will become clear in the following pages. (As a footnote to this point it is worth remembering that it was troops such as these who, when competently trained and led, did what the French and British couldn't do. They took Vimy Ridge.)

One final point. My remarks about the present-day City of Kitchener are totally personal, wholly subjective, without academic significance, and may be safely ignored.

There are many people who made this book possible. First of all there are a number of older citizens who remember the events of 1916 and the people and places involved: Wilfrid Bitzer, Junius Lockhart, Margaret Holden, Sam Weicker, Ray Woelfle, and others. Then there are the descendants of Rev. Tappert who wrote to me about their grandfather: Ruth Spitz of New Rochelle, N.Y., and J.P. Strack of Calgary. I would also like to thank the staff of the Grace Schmidt Room of the Kitchener Public Library, the Doris Lewis Rare Book Room at the University of Waterloo, and Doon Heritage Crossroads. They were all unfailingly helpful and, indeed, went out of their way to bring items of interest to my attention or show me research shortcuts that saved me many hours of work. Thanks are also due to the Canada Council for providing funding towards the publication of this work. I would also like to thank Jacqueline Underhill and Wojtek Kozlinski, who between them had the tricky job of transforming ancient photographs into acceptable prints. As

Jacqueline is also my wife she had much more than that to contend with. Her encouragement and support were invaluable.

Finally, I would like to thank Ken McLaughlin, who has been extraordinarily generous, not only with his advice and time, but also in passing along to me without reserve any information that he has collected about this period of Kitchener's history. As he is the acknowledged expert on this period, his help has been much appreciated. And I should quickly add the usual disclaimer: any errors are not his, but mine.

Waterloo, Ontario   W.R.C.
September 1992

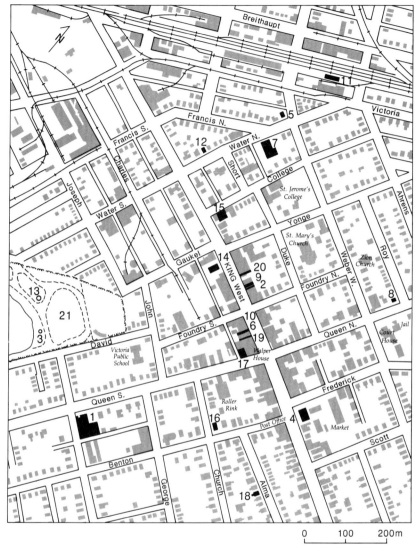

1 Barracks
2 Breithaupt's office
3 Bust of Kaiser Wilhelm I
4 City Hall
5 Cleghorn's house
6 Concordia Club
7 Dominion Button Company
8 George Lang's house
9 Gettas and Gettas
10 Grand Theatre
11 Grand Trunk Railway Station

12 Gross's house
13 Statue of Queen Victoria
14 Recruiting office
15 Roma Theatre
16 St. Matthew's Lutheran Church
17 Star Theatre
18 Tappert's house
19 The Berlin *News-Record*
20 The Berlin *Telegraph*
21 Victoria Park

The Battleground: Downtown Berlin. Based on "Map of Busy Berlin," 1912.
(Courtesy Waterloo Historical Society)

The 118th march down King St., toward the Walper House (from where this picture was taken), passing what is today Mini Mart, Knar Jewellery, Twenty King St., Jacqueline's, and so on. (Courtesy Waterloo Historical Society)

While the bells of St. Peter's Lutheran Church chimed out "God Be With You Till We Meet Again." (Courtesy Waterloo Historical Society)

Dressing for Parade. The barracks of the 118th Battalion at Courtland and Queen Streets. (Courtesy Waterloo Historical Society)

Lt. Col. W.M.O. Lochead (*fourth from right, top row*) with officers of the 118th Battalion. (Courtesy of the Schneider Corporation Archives, Norman Schneider Collection)

Square-bashing in Victoria Park under the watchful eyes
of small boys in knickerbockers and cloth caps.
(Courtesy Breithaupt-Hewetson-Clark Collection, University of Waterloo)

All that remains of the Kaiser's bust?
(Courtesy Doon Heritage Crossroads)

W.H. Breithaupt.
(Courtesy Waterloo Historical Society)

The Berlin City Council, 1915.
(Back) W.G. Cleghorn, W.E. Gallagher, D. Gross, Geo Bucher*, Dr. A.E. Rudell.
(Centre) C.C. Hahn, W.E. Trask*, J. Hessenauer, C.B. Dunke, I. Master, J.H. McCutcheon*.
(Front) Dr. H.H. Huehnergard, J.A. Hallman, Dr. J.E. Hett, Mayor, J.S. Schwartz,
Dr. J.J. Walters*. Those with a star (*) were not re-elected in 1916. Their
places were taken by J. Reid, F.K. Ferguson, G. Zettel, J.H. Schnarr.
(Courtesy Waterloo Historical Society)

S.J. Williams.
(Courtesy Grace Schmidt Room, Kitchener Public Library)

Rev. Reinhold Tappert.
(Courtesy Archives of St. Matthew's Lutheran Church)

Introduction

Kitchener's downtown core is not particularly attractive. Those who would argue differently either haven't travelled very much or else, like mothers of ill-favoured offspring, are happily blind to the flaws of that which is near and dear. This is not to say that it is an ugly city exactly. It isn't scruffy or dirty, for example, and it has no slums (or at least nothing that a Neapolitan or Mother Teresa would call a slum), and its inhabitants don't have to worry about the industrial pollution index on hot summer days. Quite the contrary. The air is pure enough to make a passing Torontonian envious, the streets gently rise and fall over the hills upon which the city is built, thus giving the potential for interesting contours and vistas, and once away from the main streets one can find sufficient trees and parks everywhere to make starlings a hazard in the Fall. And yet, for all these natural advantages, and although it is surrounded by some of the loveliest towns in Southern Ontario, Kitchener itself is about as exciting as a tool shed.

In trying to account for this curious fact one probably begins with general impressions of architecture and layout. One notices, for example, that whereas towns like Fergus and what used to be Galt are built of stone, a material that hints at permanence and dignity, Kitchener is a city of brick, and the brick is mostly of the Victorian red and pallid yellow variety. As for the buildings themselves, the gracious houses of the older residential areas, though large enough, have a fussy bric-a-brac quality about them, as though the cluttered decor of the drab nineteenth-century parlour has somehow become externalized. Many of the numerous churches are not too inspiring to look at, particularly if one compares them with, for example, the Roman Catholic cathedral in Guelph, or the two fine Presbyterian

1

churches bordering Queen's Square in Galt. To some extent a main street is a reflection of a city's soul, and here again comparisons do not flatter Kitchener. Stratford's Ontario Street, for example, has a spaciousness about it that seems to give the elbows of the mind, not to mention human beings, plenty of room to move around in, while Kitchener's downtown King Street is so cramped that it feels like a canyon into which the sun only shines at high noon.

One could probably speculate on the reasons for these differences for a long time. The cultural background of the early German settlers? Victorian sensibilities? The arrival of Scottish stonemasons and the accessibility of quarries? The colour of local clay bodies? Real estate speculations? No doubt these all played their part, but two influences (that converge and become one influence) seem to be of particular importance and deserve separate mention.

A friend once perceptively remarked that Kitchener is a city that seems to wear its business heart on its sleeve, and does so with a frankness and innocence that is quite endearing. Ken McLaughlin interestingly points out that the early factory owners liked to "live over the shop" so that they could keep an eye on the business, and that the resulting juxtaposition of industry and residence is, even today, one of Kitchener's distinguishing features. Certain it is that factories were sited uncompromisingly on main streets, railway lines ran through major intersections (and anywhere else that commerce required), and there was generally no attempt made to camouflage the sources of prosperity. In other words it was a city fired by materialistic dreams. But, it may be objected, business and commerce are what keep any big city growing, which is true. What one is talking about is a matter of ratios. Most "great" cities genuinely recognize the existence of spiritual or human or artistic values, and encourage the expression of these values through the purchase of a Henry Moore for a square, the subsidization of a theatre company, the creation of Pedestrian Only streets, and so on. But Kitchener pays only lip service, if that, to such frills. True, it built a Centre in the Square (more a Centre in the Parking Lot really), but like so many similar efforts that are fuelled by civic pomp rather than by a real understanding of community needs, it ended up with a white elephant that plays host to (apart from the K-W Symphony, a genuine achievement of real excellence) golden oldie television personalities and American touring shows, while doing relatively little to nurture local artistic efforts. But to the philistine imagination Art is simply a fancy name for Play, and Work, not Play, is the city's boast. It is also one of the reasons why, like Jack, it is a dull boy.

All this, of course, is no recent phenomenon. In the handsomely produced commemorative volume, *Berlin, Celebration of Cityhood, 1912*, the second page depicts an enthroned seraphim in workboots, clutching a sledgehammer and guarded by two lions. Beneath it is a poem by some mute, inglorious Kipling addressed "To Our Workmen In One Hundred And Twenty Factories." It canters along as follows:

Here's to the man who labours, and does it with a song!
He stimulates his neighbours and helps the world along!
I like the men who do things, who hustle and achieve;
The men who saw and glue things, and spin and dig and weave.

A nice example of Art celebrating, as it should, The Really Useful.

Dating from the same year is a panoramic photograph of Berlin that not only gives visual support to the poem, but also shows the second influence that was instrumental in fashioning the character of this city. In the foreground are factories and warehouses, sheds and sidings and rolling stock, and the billowing curve of the railway tracks distorted by the primitive camera—much of it still in existence. The middleground is punctuated by industrial chimneys and behind them are clearly visible the spires and towers of churches. Not remarkable, one might say, for a view of any town; but in this case it is a nice reminder that religion, in a very special sense, lies behind the birth of the community. Here the church didn't follow the settler. The church was the settler.

Religion and business. The idealist might suppose these to be opposites, but of course they are not, for an alliance of commerce and theology in which the blessings of the latter sanctify the efforts of the former has always been the essence of colonial enterprises. Today, the religious justification has become superfluous, but in the early 1900s the marriage of church and capitalism was important and in Berlin, Ontario, it was probably as full, perfect, and sufficient as anywhere in the world. Another piece of literature from the commemorative volume already mentioned illustrates the point. It occupies a full page, is surrounded by a wreathed border of leaves and roses, is printed in 24-point Gothic lettering, and contains not the faintest whiff of parody or self-consciousness. It is titled "My Creed":

I believe in Berlin. I love her as my home. I honor her institutions. I rejoice in the abundance of her resources. I have unbounded confidence in the ability and enterprise of her people, and I cherish exalted ideas of her destiny among cities of the Dominion.

Anything that is produced in Berlin, from Canadian materials, by the application of Canadian brain and labor, will always have first call with me. And it's only good business on my part that it should.

In other words, Berlin was fashioned, not by an aesthetic, but by a work ethic that could be expressed with the cheerful piety of a biblical faith. In 1912 it was as hard-working, religious, law-abiding, and confident a city as any in the Dominion, and there was no reason to believe that the future would ever be different.

ONE

Background to War

The consequences of a particular historical event thread their way down through the ages, multiplying organically, until in the fullness of time they issue in other events that appear to have little in common with the "first cause."

In Switzerland in 1525, Conrad Grebel had a bitter falling out with Huldrych Zwingli over a matter of profound religious importance to both men. As a result of this dispute, about 400 years later a small Ontario town tore itself apart on the apparently insignificant question of whether or not it should change its name. The earlier argument was the more ferocious of the two because it involved matters of high principle; it led to martyrdoms, persecutions, and hardships, and it stands as a testament to the resilience of the human spirit. It is a history that people wish to remember. The later argument was an undignified affair; it may have caused no deaths, but it also created no faiths because no great principles were involved. It is the sort of history people try to forget.

This is an account of what actually happened in Berlin, Ontario, between November 1, 1915, and January 1, 1917. It is the story of how a city of solid, hard-working people became nationally known as a place where law and order had broken down, where it was dangerous to walk the main streets in daylight, where clubs and shops were wrecked by mobs, a clergyman and his family were assaulted in their own home, and a mayor-elect was advised by the military authorities to "go to some friend's house . . . and there keep quiet and let no one know [your] whereabouts." The framework to these events is a world at war; the picture is that of a city at war.

All this was 75 years ago, and the city has long since reassumed its mask of sober, middle-class respectability, but for a

5

long time the unfortunate events of 1915 and 1916 were treated as a family secret that it was best not to talk about, especially when outsiders were present. Mabel Dunham, for example, in *Grand River* (1945) talks of "whisperings, silly prejudices, bitter racial hatred and faults on both sides," but prefers to draw a decent veil over the details. She wishes that "those terrible days might be blotted out of the great book of remembrance," but doesn't tell us what it is that we don't want to remember. A little earlier, W.V. Uttley, in *A History of Kitchener, Ontario* (1937), befogged the issue even more effectively.

> For the majority of citizens, war-time was a period of trial, yet stamped with exemplary conduct. . . . In 1916, reports of the criticisms levelled at Sir Adam Beck on account of his German parentage reached the city. Fearing that Berlin might be next, two hundred businessmen petitioned the council to change the name of the city. That was finally done. . . . Of the break, native-born citizens said in effect, we deplore the change but must accept it.

That does not, one might say, quite tell the whole story.

More recently, three excellent studies have included sections that describe, without pulling any punches, the sequence of events of 1916 in Berlin. These are *Kitchener: An Illustrated History* (1983) by John English and Kenneth McLaughlin, *The Kaiser's Bust* (1991) by Patricia McKegney, and *Ontario and the First World War* (1977) by Barbara Wilson. What this book hopes to do is add some further details to the story, to supply some shading to the bare outlines, and perhaps above all to try to bring back to life to some extent the men and women who had their exits and their entrances in this little scene of history. If these people begin to take on the roles of heroes and villains, of clowns and wise counsellors, well, perhaps that is only natural in a story as dramatic as this one.

It is difficult to say whether looking at the skeletons in our closets is a useful exercise or not. Sometimes what we learn translates into a wisdom that helps to shape present and future events. Sometimes it translates into a superiority of the "It couldn't possibly happen today" variety—a superiority that has a habit of collapsing when it happens today. But history is its own justification. It survives, to misquote Auden, in the valley of its doing, and all we can do is try to find out what happened and how it came about. For the purposes of the present book I have suggested that Zurich, Switzerland, in 1525 is the proper starting point.

There was nothing monolithic about the development of the Reformation in Europe. Although all Protestant coats were ostensibly cut from the same simple materials and shaped to an earlier design, there was much disagreement about what the earlier design was, not to mention how the coats should be worn. Ironically, these disagreements sometimes resulted in animosities as virulent as those that were directed against the tattered finery of Rome. In 1522, Zwingli, who had been preaching Luther's new-fangled ideas, made a convert of a young, easygoing humanist called Conrad Grebel. For a time the two were like father and son, but as has often happened in like circumstances both before and since, the younger man, perhaps in order to atone for past errors, became a more zealous and impatient reformer than his mentor, and a schism gradually developed between them. Among the beliefs about which they argued were infant baptism and, more significantly for our story, the use of force, both of which Grebel rejected.

Matters came to a head in a great debate before the Council of Zurich on January 17, 1525, which Zwingli officially "won," and on the next day the persecution of Grebel and his followers began. But if Zwingli had been more sensitive to the lessons of history he might perhaps have realized that persecution is a fine fertilizer for the growth of healthy religions. Certain it is that this attack by Protestant on Protestant marks the beginning of the Anabaptist movement and was also the cause of its early dissemination into South Germany and Austria, as the first of Grebel's followers (better known today by the names of the sects into which they later subdivided—Mennonites, Hutterites, Amish) sought to find a land where they would be free to live and worship in peace.

About five years after these events in Switzerland a similar movement arose in the Netherlands. Whether Dutch Anabaptism was the direct result of proselytizing from the south, or whether it arose more or less independently from the general swirl of religious thought that was eddying about Europe at the time is hard to say, but the new faith flourished even more vigorously in the north in spite of, or maybe because of, the inevitable martyrdoms—perhaps 2,500 burnings, beheadings, hangings, etc., in the first 60 years. The most important early leader of the Dutch Anabaptists was Menno Simons who, remarkably, man-

aged to die of natural causes at the age of 65. He was the theor-
ist of the movement, wrote several treatises about its beliefs,
carried its gospel in person into the States of Upper Germany
and, of course, gave his name to one of its main sects.

The Mennonites might aptly be called the Jews of Christian-
ity, for their history right up to the present century seems to
have consisted of a succession of diasporas. These scatterings
follow a well-defined pattern. A number of families would first
of all move to a state or country that promised them safety from
oppression and freedom to conduct their lives in accordance
with their beliefs. Here they would initially be welcomed by the
authorities, who would be delighted to count such a peace-
loving and hard-working people amongst their subjects. Then,
after decades of prosperity and an increase in the number of
congregations, either there would be no more land available for
expansion or their policy of segregation would arouse those animosities that stem from jealousy and suspicion or, more likely,
there would be an attempt to impose laws on them that were
unacceptable to their their religious beliefs — military service,
oath-taking, and the like. And so it would come time to move on
again and for the cycle to be repeated once more. In this way
the Mennonites spread outwards from their two initial starting
points of Switzerland and Holland, first to most of the states of
Germany, next to Austria and Hungary, then eastwards into
Poland and Russia, and finally into North and South America.

The first Mennonites seem to have reached North America in
the 1640s, but these earliest arrivals were probably part of the
general exploration movement of the new continent, and they
established no communities.

1n 1662, Cornelius Plockhoy started a Mennonite colony in
New Amsterdam, but his utopian aspirations didn't take into
consideration the imperialist squabbles of the European superpowers (in this case the English and the Dutch) so that when, in
1664, an English force invaded the Dutch colonies of the Dela-
ware, Plockhoy's village, along with other settlements, was
reduced "to a naile." History, however, is full of little ironies,
and some 20 years later the first permanent Mennonite settlement was firmly planted in the New World. It was not far from
Plockhoy's nail, and this time it was courtesy of the English.

The man responsible for this reversal was the aristocratic
and handsome William Penn, who became a Quaker when he was
22 and thereafter preached the peaceful Quaker way of life with

remarkable energy, tenacity and, one is almost tempted to say, belligerence. In 1681, the perennially impecunious Charles II paid off a debt to the Penn family by giving William a worthless chunk of American real estate (about the size of England), and it was here that Penn determined to launch what he called his "Holy Experiment" – a state where all citizens would be free to worship as they chose. High on his list of preferred colonizers were the Mennonites (many of whose congregations he had visited on his trips to Europe), not only because they were an oppressed religious group whose beliefs were in many ways similar to those of the Quakers, but also because, from a strictly business point of view, their honesty and their capacity for hard work made them the perfect tenants.

The original 13 families who sailed across the Atlantic on the *Concord* in 1683 settled at Germantown, now a part of Philadelphia. This first trickle of Mennonite immigration soon became a steady stream, and by the middle of the eighteenth century their numbers had increased to between 3,000 and 5,000 souls. The first arrivals came from the north of Germany and then, after 1707, more often from the Palatinate and Switzerland; but wherever they came from they all spoke a German dialect of one sort or another, and together with the many thousands of other Germans of different faiths, created a distinctive regional culture that is known today as Pennsylvania Dutch or, more correctly, *Deutsch*.

As might be expected, the Mennonites prospered mightily in the new land, whether as merchants, artisans or farmers, and as they prospered they fanned out from Philadelphia into the counties of south-west Pennsylvania. The future looked promising but, as had happened so often before, this peaceful expansion was soon threatened by external events which, though of no great intrinsic interest to the Mennonites, would cause some of them to set off on their travels once again. This time the direction would be northwards, travelling by foot and on long sway-backed wagons to a wilderness relatively devoid of civilized life and about which information could only be transmitted as rumour.

The American War of Independence (1775-83) caught the Mennonites in their perennial dilemma, though this time they found themselves between two competing sides, both of which expected their support, whether real or tacit. For the Mennonites the balance was more or less equally weighted. Certainly they had no strong desire to assist an insurrection against an authority that had treated them reasonably fairly over the years, while the American rebels for their part were a mite suspicious of a people who refused to participate in what was obviously a just cause, who probably sympathized with their revolutionary ideals but were prepared to let someone else do the bloody work, and who, finally, were of the same culture and spoke the same language as many of the soldiers that the stout German king of England had sent to fight against them. (The Germans were nothing if not ubiquitous in the eighteenth century, their influence stretching from the farmlands of North America to the throne of England.) These feelings led to a bit of harassment of the Mennonites in Pennsylvania, and although it was not by any means persecution in the grand European manner, it served to ruffle a few feathers. But the other side of the coin is also pertinent. As historians have pointed out, the whole thrust of the Independence movement was to gain freedom from an external tyranny and to maintain the principle that all humans were created equal and should be able to enjoy such inalienable rights as the preservation of life, liberty, and the pursuit of happiness. And what Mennonite could disagree with those sentiments! But then maybe some of them were aware of the gap that frequently exists between the sonorous phrase and the stark fact, and that even while the rhetoric rolled from Jefferson's lips, his estates back in Virginia were being worked by a hundred black slaves.

Though it would be pleasant to believe that those Mennonites who quit America during the war years did so because, like some early version of United Empire Loyalists, the Union Jack fluttered in their breasts (and some may have been so motivated), the fact that the majority of their brethren remained where they were in Pennsylvania and adapted quite happily to the new order of things suggests that there were other reasons involved. By far the most important of these was, quite simply, land hunger. The Mennonites tended to have healthy families, and as each unit grew and prospered, the rising generations had to look elsewhere for their farmland. They could, of course, try to buy in populous Pennsylvania, but with prices reaching the absurd height of $100 an acre, prospects were dim for those trying to get established. Thus when the British government began offering land for two or three dollars an acre to loyalists, the combination of inducements was irresistible. That the land so offered was way up north in a place called Canada, which a dastardly rumour claimed was Portuguese for "nothing here," was neither here nor there. Taming the wilderness was the name of the game in those days, and the first conestoga wagons began to lurch and bump their way towards this unknown territory in 1786.

Although not one of the epic migrations of the world, the journey that the Mennonites undertook from Pennsylvania to Ontario deserves an honourable mention in the People against Nature category. As journeys went it was not particularly dangerous (or at least not in comparison with the Atlantic crossings of their ancestors when Death regularly claimed a portion of the human cargo) or that long (some 400 miles), but it still required enormous stamina and courage from those who wished to make it.

Typically the route ran up the valley of the Susquehanna until it petered out in the foothills of the first serious obstacle, the Allegheny Mountains. Once up and over these the travellers made a left-hand sweep in the vicinity of Rochester and so on to a second and even more impressive barrier, the Niagara River, with its falls and rapids. Here the conestoga wagons were converted into rafts which were winched across the dangerous waters by means of ropes and pulleys. Once in the new country it was a matter of trundling westwards — basically following what is today the Q.E.W. — with Lake Ontario on the right-hand side and the Niagara escarpment towering up on the left all the way to present-day Hamilton. At this point there was the option of either cutting over to the valley of the Grand River and so north-westwards again or, if one were intrepid and wanted to shorten the trip by 30 miles or so, heading north right away, which meant going through the Beverley Swamp where, as likely as not, the wagons would get stuck. If that happened there was nothing for it but to unload all the family goods and chattels, take the wagon apart piece by piece, carry everything by hand several hundred yards to firmer ground, presumably slapping wildly at the mosquitoes all the while, reassemble the wagon once more, reload, and so push on until the next stoppage. One is inclined to think that a canoe portage is child's play compared to a conestoga portage, but the Mennonites, whether they tried the Beverley Swamp route or not, had to undertake the frustrating operation more than once on their long journey.

The first Mennonites to cross the Niagara only continued on for a few more miles along the shores of Lake Ontario before stopping in what is today the Vineland-Jordan area. Here, at the Twenty as it was called, a settlement grew up which was able to give encouragement and assistance to later arrivals to Upper

Canada, and to act as a last staging post for those who in increasing numbers pushed on for another 55 miles into that uninhabited interior which was to be the latest in a series of Promised Lands.

The story of the settlement of Waterloo County has been told many times and is now approaching the status of myth. If not fairytale. Or melodrama. Virtually all the elements are there: the wicked landlord, the simple country lad, the deception, the impossible task, the quest undertaken, the journey successful, and innocence triumphant. There is as yet no maiden threatened with a fate worse than death, but perhaps future generations will rectify the omission. Alas, the real story (the edges of which are still a bit fuzzy) was a little more mundane and seems to have included good old-fashioned flip-flopping of land for profit by all concerned.

The man to whom legend assigned the role of villain was a Colonel Richard Beasley. He purchased some 90,000 acres of Six Nations reserve land from Joseph Brant for about £9,000. Beasley was obviously hoping to sell off this land in order to finance his purchase, even though he had promised not to do so until the mortgage had been cleared. His first sales were to members of the unworldy looking religious sect that began to appear in his neck of the woods in 1800 and who he assumed wouldn't ask too many questions. The Mennonites, however, quickly discovered that the clear titles they thought they had purchased were still under a mortgage, and a certain amount of consternation ensued. Subsequently, a small group (Brickers and Erbs) agreed with Beasley to purchase 60,000 acres for some £11,000 and paid nearly half of this amount down. They agreed to pay off the balance within two years, their intention being to dispose of lots to other incoming Mennonites and, in the process, like Beasley, turn a tidy profit. However, on the date stipulated they still didn't have the money, and Colonel Claus, the chairman of the trustees of the Six Nations, a government body that was trying to ride herd on the Indians' feckless desire to sell off their reserve lands (or maybe Brant was also making a dollar or two on the side), gave them one more year to come up with the principal or else lose their already considerable investment.

It is at this point that legend may be allowed to kick in. Faced with the need to raise a sum of money too large for a local whip-round, Samuel Bricker and Joseph Sherk rode back to Pennsylvania and, after much speechifying and exhortation, persuaded their well-to-do brethren to put up the required cash in return for the creation of a Land Company in which all would have shares. The money was duly collected in silver coin, put into 200 canvas bags, placed in a wagon and, accompanied by a few men (needless to say unarmed), calmly driven the 400 miles back to Ontario. This cheeky method of transferring huge sums of money worked for the Mennonites not once, but two or three times, and only goes to show that when God is on your side who needs Brinks.

The Mennonites now had 60,000 acres of land to dispose of, and the next two decades saw a large number of the faithful flooding into Waterloo Township, clearing, building, and putting down roots. One such was Joseph Schneider, who took up Lot 17, and who, in 1807, erected a log cabin at the foot of one of the sandy hills which were a feature of his property. This cabin was the first building in what soon became a thriving little village — though why this particular piece of real estate should become a village, let alone a thriving one, is hard to figure out. It wasn't on a river like Galt or Fergus or Elora, the Grand being a mile or so to the east; it wasn't on much of a road to anywhere; and it didn't sit on a prominence from whence it could view the surrounding countryside. What it did have was sand, which blew everywhere when it was dry, and cedar swamp that made life soggy when it was wet. In the list of unlikely sites for settlement, only Regina surpasses it.

Shortly after this the Mennonite contribution to our story begins to come to an end. By 1825 (300 years after that fiery dispute in Zurich), the emigration from Pennsylvania had just about come to an end, and from now on the new arrivals to the growing community came from other sources. Not surprisingly, the majority of them came from the German states, from Brandenburg, from Hesse, from Saxony and Baden, from Westphalia and Mecklenburg, all of them attracted to the idea of starting life anew in a place where their own language was already the dominant one and where their culture and traditions would be understood and respected. The Mennonites for their part welcomed these new arrivals who were, like themselves, thrifty and hard-working, and most of whom were skilled artisans into the bargain.

But before taking leave of the Mennonites, two more legacies, one intangible, the other concrete, both of them of the utmost importance to this history, need to be mentioned. The first was the sect's already-mentioned insistence on non-violence and non-involvement, and here one gets the feeling that somehow these beliefs continued to float in the air of the county long after the Mennonites themselves had ceased to be a numerical majority or have any social influence. Perhaps they could be said to have established a tradition—though a later recruiting sergeant would have called it something else—albeit a tradition that was absolutely in tune with the dreams of the new settlers, most of whom had consciously sought a place where "nor war or battle's sound was heard."

Secondly, there was the matter of a name. What should the village that had been founded in this unpromising spot be called? The earliest choice seems to have been the attractively descriptive one of Sand Hills, but shortly another name began to vie with it in popularity, a name that was intended to honour the village's most respected inhabitant, Benjamin Eby. Like Schneider, Eby had arrived in 1807, and purchased Lot 2, which was the next-door piece of land, and thus also a part of the village. He soon showed himself to be a man of learning, leadership, and spiritual grace. In 1809 he became the congregation's preacher and, in 1812, their bishop. Shortly thereafter the name Ebytown was proposed for the tiny settlement. Unfortunately, the good bishop seems to have counted modesty amongst his many virtues, and he suggested (one speculates) that a name less embarrassingly personal would be more appropriate; a name perhaps that would acknowledge the contributions that the new arrivals were making to the community and also be a pleasant reminder for them of the country they had left behind. It was a nice gesture, but future events lead one to wish that Eby had been less humble. One obvious choice for the new name was that of the capital city of the state of Prussia, a city that was fast becoming one of the liveliest commercial and cultural centres in Europe, a city that, as Modris Eksteins says in *Rites of Spring*, "made all its visitors instantly aware of newness and vitality" (p. 73). The adoption of its name would surely bestow an innocent touch of dignity on the multiplying cluster of log cabins in the middle of darkest Upper Canada and suggest the confident aspirations of those who lived in them. The fact that the European city was also by this time becoming something of a military centre was not perceived to be significant. In 1833 Schneider and Eby agreed on the name Berlin.

Due to the social and political unrest that continued to be a part of the European scene for some decades, German emigration into Waterloo Township increased through the middle of the nineteenth century. As has been suggested, it is unlikely that these emigrants were militantly concerned with nationalism, liberalism, unification or any other popular nineteenth-century cause. If they had been they probably wouldn't have left. To the contrary, they were people who were tired of excessive taxation, long years of compulsory military service, and not knowing from one year to the next whether an army or two would demolish their crops or plunder their shops. All they wanted was to get out and find a place where life could be lived in peace. In other words they were not fighters of causes, but workers and artisans; their impulses were to avoid confrontations, to get on with the job, and to improve themselves materially. These, then, were the settlers who, in 1871, were instrumental in changing Berlin from a village into a town (ironically the same year that Berlin became the capital of a unified Germany), and later into a city (1912). They gave the place its personality, a personality that is summarized in its proud motto — Busy Berlin.

But it would be a mistake to think of Berlin as exclusively German right through the nineteenth century. As the town grew and prospered the Anglo-Saxons began to put in an appearance, predominately, perhaps, the Scots, who played such a large part in building the encircling towns, but also the English, Welsh, and Irish. And, not surprisingly, it was the British who often occupied the more influential governmental and professional positions in the town. Upper Canada was, after all, a British colony and remained so in all but a strictly political sense long after 1867, and since knowledge of the English language controlled entrance into the professions and into the realms of officialdom, the German speaker was initially at a disadvantage. Add to this the fact that the town's founding fathers were opposed to holding public office and that the majority of the later immigrants worked with their hands rather than their heads, and one can see how the British played a more influential role in the life of the community than their original, nearly nonexistent, contribution warranted.

But if this was the situation in the middle decades of the century, by 1900, when second- and third-generation German-Canadians were a commonplace, and only a person's name indicated family origin, such distinctions had become largely blurred. Those of German background remained very much in the majority at the turn of the century of course (70% to 80% of all public school students still studied German as one of their optional subjects — until, that is, the school board abolished the teaching of German in 1915 on the pretext that it overburdened the youthful mind), but now a doctor was as likely to be a Honsberger as a Smith, and a labourer at the factory bench a Jones as a Schantz. And to complicate matters further, Honsberger and Schantz were as likely to have voted for the abolition of the teaching of German as Smith or Jones. Indeed, in the case just mentioned, the majority of the school trustees were of German descent; although it should be added that external pressures by that time were warping actions in strange ways.

But if all were more or less united under the banner of Civic Pride, and pursued together the common goals of making money, leading the good life, and worshipping God (in German for the vast majority) on Sunday, there was still no doubt that the city was built on two different cultures. For the British this posed no problems; all their allegiances streamed unquestioningly across the ocean to our dear Queen and all she stood for. But for the Germans of whatever generation, loyalties were split; on the one hand there was their superb cultural heritage — food, dress, language, literature, music, art — to which they were rightly attached; and on the other, for most, there was the government, the monarchy, and the flag of the country that had given their ancestors refuge and ensured their own human rights.

Perhaps the divided and distinguished world of Berlin was to some extent symbolized by the opening of Victoria Park in 1896. It may have been dedicated to "her," but interestingly enough the first statue to be placed in it was a bronze bust of Kaiser Wilhelm I. Still, as an English family eating their meat-paste sandwiches on the grass beside the lake might have remarked to the German family sitting beside them, "What does it matter? After all, the walrus-faced gentleman with the fluffy mutton chops is father-in-law to the dear queen's eldest, isn't he? It's all in the family. Would you like a meat-paste sandwich?" And as the German family, politely declining the offer, might have replied, "Yes, indeed, they're really all Germans, aren't they. Would you like a slice of *Kuchen*?" But maybe this picture of bucolic friendship and mutual indifference to world affairs is too naive. Perhaps the anonymous "Group of Citizens" who subscribed to Wilhelm's statue were more than a little aware that he was the first emperor of the modern, united Germany, that under his chancellor, Bismarck, Germany had become a world power, and that his own overriding interest lay in the development of his beloved army. Certainly one gets the impression of a political counter-statement being belatedly made when, 12 years later, a slightly taller, full-length statue of Queen Victoria herself was erected a short distance away, courtesy of the Imperial Order of the Daughters of the (British) Empire.

And by now it must have been faintly discernible, even to a bustling and supremely confident Ontario city of some 16,000 souls, that events were occurring offstage that were a cause for uneasiness, and those Berliners who were both perceptive and pessimistic must have wondered whether their own city, with its unique background and composition, might not be in for a particularly rough ride. The pessimists were, of course, proved right. In 1914, the European superpowers decided once more that it was time to sort each other out, and in the hot summer of that year the prolix headlines of the Berlin *News-Record* chanted the countdown to destruction:

Wednesday, July 29	War Cloud In Europe Has Broken And Fighting Along The Border Between Austria And Servia Is In Progress
Thursday, July 30	War Has Actually Begun Between The Artillery Near Semendria On Servian Soil
Friday, July 31	Only A Miracle Can Prevent An All Around Conflict In Europe
Saturday, August 1	Strenuous Efforts By Britain, Germany And France To Avoid A General War
Monday, August 3	War To The Death Has Come To Europe
Tuesday, August 4	Great Britain Has Not Declared War
Wednesday, August 5	Germany Declares War On England England Declares War On Germany

For many a family in Berlin, Ontario, that final headline must have caused feelings of real confusion.

TWO

How to Raise a Battalion

As often as not a stupid war is greeted with mindless euphoria and a necessary one with soberness and regret. World War I was such a war, and the universal delight with which it opened was heightened by the conviction that the whole picnic wouldn't last long anyway. For the Allies it was "business as usual," and "We'll be home before Christmas," and in *Punch* the cartoon rogue requested His Lordship to put him away for six months or the duration of the war. For the beautifully efficient German war machine it was going to be even shorter. In and out of Paris in about two weeks, and mop up the rest of Europe in maybe six more.

Unfortunately, everybody had got hold of the wrong time-table, and as early as the first winter it was clear that a very different sort of campaign was taking shape. Instead of swift troop movements by train and truck, plus scintillating cavalry charges hither and yon, trenches began to be dug, and then trenches to support trenches, and then yet more trenches to support these. Next it was a question of gift-wrapping all the trenches in barbed wire, destroying every tree, bush, and blade of grass in sight, and finally waiting for the rain to fall. Which it did in copious amounts. Soon there was an incredible network of soggy ditch and dripping wire stretching all the way from the English Channel in the north to the Vosges Mountains in the south, and here the armies came to a halt. It was stasis in the mud. And for the next four years a generation of young men, urged on by their leaders, slowly wiped each other out in the most horrifying war the world had yet seen.

In the circumstances it was not surprising that bellicosity, in all its simplistic dullness, soon turned into more interesting emotional mixtures, particularly for the soldiers at the Front — cynicism, helplessness, fortitude, terror, joy, and hilarity all rolled into one — and that by the first Christmas, when the troops from both sides walked into No Man's Land to exchange gifts with each other, the songs of the army were beginning to reflect the new spirit. The old, patriotic tub-thumpers of earlier wars such as,

> We don't want to fight, but by jingo if we do,
> We've got the ships, we've got the men, and got the money too,

had had their words changed to

> I don't want to fight, I'll be slaughtered if I do.
> I'll change my togs, I'll sell my kit and pop my rifle too,

while even that most popular marching song of them all not only challenged the foot slogger to pack up his troubles in his old kit bag and stop worrying, it also exhorted him, with suspicious frequency, to smile — no less than seven times in each chorus.

And by that first Christmas, too, it was patently obvious that hundreds of thousands more Private Perks would have to be issued with old kit bags than had originally been estimated. The pre-war, professional army of 100,000 men that had constituted the British Expeditionary Force had been decimated, as had the first infusion of volunteers, and this was not surprising when one considers that the aggressive German army consisted of over 4,000,000 well-trained men. Indeed, it was only French stubbornness, Russian belligerence, and human error that had saved the day. Inevitably the cry was for more and more men to feed the monster, whose appetite for human flesh was beginning to seem insatiable. By October of 1915 the official British casualties stood at 493,294, and without a doubt the other participants in the "ever popular War Game" could claim that their own scores were every bit as good,

In England, the original target of six divisions, which most warlords had assumed would be sufficient for the task ahead, was revised upwards. To 70 divisions. This meant more serious recruiting methods (conscription didn't become law until May 1916), which in turn meant dusting off those noble techniques of persuasion that emphasized blandishment and moral blackmail. In the publicity campaign that ensued, the mother country was fortunate to possess a superb recruiting sergeant in its secretary of state for war, the magnetic, six-foot, six-inch national hero with the glorious moustaches and piercing eyes, Lord Kitchener of Omdurman. Soon the impressive head was staring out from the famous recruiting poster, and the minatory finger was inducing 3,000,000 civilians to swap their brollies for rifles. But 3,000,000 was only the British contribution; the call for recruits was intended for the whole of the far-flung Empire, so that it was not long before Kitchener's finger had crept across the Atlantic to tickle the conscience of the Dominion of Canada.

In 1915, then, the desultory volunteering that had constituted this country's war effort began to change in tone and tempo. On October 22, George V added his voice to Kitchener's in a regal, though clumsily worded, message that went round the globe and was printed in Berlin's two daily newspapers.

> To My People: At this grave moment in the struggle between my people and a highly organized enemy, who has transgressed the laws of nations and changed the ordinance that binds civilized Europe together, I appeal to you.
>
> I rejoice in my Empire's effort, and I feel pride in the voluntary response from my subjects all over the world, who have sacrificed home and future and life in order that another may not inherit the free Empire which their ancestors and mine have built. I ask you to make good those sacrifices.
>
> The end is not in sight. More men, and yet more are wanted to keep my armies in the field, and through them to secure victory and an enduring peace.

One week later, on October 29, Canada responded directly to the royal plea with a promise to raise its commitment to 250,000 men, or 10 divisions, and no doubt the news helped to ease the physical discomfort of the king who, the day before, had fallen off his horse while reviewing his troops.

As far as Canada was concerned it was simply a matter of finding the balance of 250,000 men (an encouraging number had already enlisted, but presumably that meant that the rest would need a bit of persuading), and the obvious first step was to invite offers of support from municipalities across the country; it would, of course, be at the local level that the raising of a volunteer army would succeed or fail. Within 24 hours of the request being made, representatives of 17 areas, from Nova Scotia to British Columbia, had responded. Amongst these was W.G. Weichel, the Conservative M.P. for Waterloo North, whose promptness in offering loyal support may not have been uncon-

nected with his sensitivity to the ancestry of so many of his electors, or even to his own ancestry. Both his parents had been
born in Germany. Whatever the reason, Weichel was one of the
first to inform Sir Sam Hughes, the minister of militia, that his
constituency would be delighted to help out. Unfortunately, he
seems not to have stipulated the exact size of a possible contribution, but to have referred vaguely to "one or two regiments."
He also forgot that Hughes, the ebullient, not to say braggado-
cio, captain of the Canadian war effort had an imagination similar to a grain of mustard seed — it had a tendency to luxuriant
growth from small beginnings. As the Berlin *Telegraph* commented after one of his grandiose pronouncements: "The only
thing that prevents Major General Sir Sam Hughes from writing
as good bulletins in Canada as Napoleon Bonaparte did in Egypt
is that there are no pyramids in this country to tack them to."
Needless to say, Hughes accepted Weichel's offer with delight
and promptly translated it into two full battalions as a good,
round contribution from Waterloo County. It was probably this
initial overestimation of the county's recruitment potential, an
overestimation based on no realistic appraisal at all of its ethnic
origins and composition, that was one of the root causes of the
trouble to come.

The news that Waterloo County had been pledged for two
battalions for overseas service came quickly down the pipeline
to Lt. Colonel H.J. Bowman, the elderly founder and commander of Berlin's "home guard," the 108th Regiment, and he
decided to make the momentous announcement (which had
already been leaked to the press) the following day. As luck
would have it, the Star Theatre had planned a three-night drive
to stimulate recruiting, and box-office sales, and this seemed to
Bowman a good opportunity for reading his letter from Hughes
to the public. Bowman's own excitement was increased by the
hope that he himself might be the commander of the new overseas outfit, although within a few days he was passed over for a
younger man from his regiment.

It was, then, on a cold Monday evening, November 1, 1915,
that the war, which till now had been a distant reality gleaned
from newspapers, finally became a more immediate presence in
Berlin. To the thump and twirl of martial music, the 108th Regiment came swinging through the dusk down King Street on its
way to the Star Theatre, drawing to them, like seagulls to a
returning fishing boat, the inevitable crowd of small boys, plus
blasé adults trying to pretend they were going in the same direc-

tion anyway. King Street was to witness many more such parades in the months ahead, as well as other scenes of a much less pleasant nature. The militia was in high spirits, possibly because they were being admitted free (otherwise, adults 10¢, children 5¢), and they all gathered in the balcony, from which vantage point they could operate as an effective cheering section. The evening's program was the usual patriotic mixed grill. There were a number of "shorts" interspersed with community singing of cheerful war songs; there was a longer movie called *The Ordeal*, billed as the greatest recruiting movie of all time and featuring Jean Renyea being tortured to death for the motherland in the Franco-Prussian War; there was an exhortatory sermon on the text of "The Just Cause" from Rev. Dr. Marcus Scott of St. Andrew's Presbyterian Church, who allowed as how his one regret was that he couldn't just don the khaki and get to the Front himself; and there were moving appeals from wounded veterans, who were at this time something of a novelty in Berlin. On this latter element of the night's entertainment, a letter to the *News-Record* the next day wondered whether seeing wrecked men swathed in bandages and plaster moving haltingly onto the platform with the aid of canes and crutches was such a great recruiting idea. And finally, as a grand climax, there was Colonel Bowman and his letter, the contents of which were greeted with the rapturous applause that one would expect on such a heady evening.

But the shouting and the cheering had barely died away before more sober second thoughts began to surface. Maybe two complete battalions was a rather tall order for what was quite openly termed the German County, and the tentative suggestion was made that perhaps one overseas battalion, built around the already existing 71st Regiment at Galt, might be a more realistic proposition. At almost the same time, however, the military interests in South Waterloo, which included the heavily Scottish towns of Preston and Galt, petitioned to be allowed to raise one of the two battalions on their own, and this was agreed to. Whether their request stemmed from genuine local pride or from a canny assessment of where recruiting potential really lay, the result was disastrous for North Waterloo, which was the heavily German part of the county and which was now lumbered with raising a battalion by itself. One person to whom such worries had occurred was Major W.M.O. Lochead, who had been transferred from the 108th to create and command the as yet non-existent battalion.

Lochead, who was 41 at the time, was an extremely personable gentleman with a lean, perhaps even ascetic, face. Though he had not perhaps climbed the ladder of success quite as high as some, as the Berlin agent for Mutual Life he knew everyone in town worth knowing and was well liked by most of them. Indeed, during most of the period covered by this history he combined his military office with the presidency of the Berlin Board of Trade, the ancestor of the Chamber of Commerce. His office was on King Street, just past Foundry, though he himself preferred to live in Waterloo. Whether his ability to marshall insurance policies, make contacts, and play at soldier was adequate training for the sterner job of commanding a professional military unit was yet to be seen.

Early in November Lochead travelled to Ottawa to put some of his concerns about recruiting to the minister of militia. Sir Sam's response was typical. He grandly brushed Lochead's reservations aside, elevated him to the rank of Lieutenant Colonel on the spot and, as an extra sop, tossed North Wellington into his recruiting catchment area. The addition of North Wellington really meant little more than the addition of a large number of Mennonite-owned farms, and Lochead already had plenty of those in North Waterloo, but the area looked sizeable enough, and this helped to allay fears somewhat. Besides, for a battalion one only needed 1,100 men, and as Colonel Bowman pointed out after some swift figuring with rules-of-thumb and statistics, if 1 in 10 members of any population may be deemed of recruitable age, and if this figure is divided into the total population of the catchment area, then there were 3,500 young men somewhere out there waiting to be cajoled into the 118th. Surely a sufficient margin for religious beliefs, romantic attachments, Oedipus complexes, cowardice, and other obstacles to patriotism.

Anyway, it was too late for doubts now. Sir Sam wanted a battalion, and North Waterloo had committed itself to one. It had a number: the 118th of the Canadian Expeditionary Force. It had a commanding officer. It even had about a dozen recruits. It was now up to local initiative to set up an organization that would produce 1,088 more.

The first step was obviously to hold a meeting, and this was arranged for Monday evening, November 8, in the Council Chamber of Berlin's city hall at the corner of King and Frederick, where Market Square now stands. The meeting, open to all interested parties, got off to an inauspicious start. It had been called for 8 p.m., but at that hour nobody had arrived. Then, when people began drifting in, it was realized that Monday nights were also drill nights, which meant that there would be almost no representation from the military. Furthermore, Lou McBrine, who had agreed to chair this initial get-together, had suddenly dashed off to Toronto in order to look after the interests of his luggage business. His regrets were brought and his place was taken by his partner (i/c Sales), W.G. Cleghorn.

Cleghorn, one of the major actors in this drama, was a small man of 53. He had been born in Scotland and therefore was affectionately, though not very originally, known as Scotty. Perhaps it is this provenance that suggests the Highland terrier in his flat head and neatly clipped hair and moustache, and his actions in 1916 show that he certainly had some of the characteristics of the breed. As well as being vice-president of McBrine Leather, he was also an alderman, having scraped in 13th out of 15 in the 1915 civic elections (he improved this to 10th in the 1916 vote).

Cleghorn began the proceedings by asking whether perhaps they shouldn't postpone the meeting to another day, as it was getting a bit late, but the consensus seemed to be that now that they were all there they should press on. But how to press on? Nobody had tried to raise an army before, and the rituals involved were a bit fuzzy. A few shy and fitful suggestions were thrown into the ring. What about recruiting in the streets? And what about the country districts? How about bringing in some outside speakers? George DeBus, a young man whose flamboyant waxed moustaches spiked the air well past the sides of his round cheeks, thereby making him a walking advertisement for his gleaming "tonsorial parlour" on King Street just across the road from the Walper House, was confused. The Board of Trade, of which he was an executive member, had just endorsed the idea of raising troops for the 108th. Now they were going to raise troops for the 118th. Which was it to be? Or was it to be both at once? No one was quite sure, but perhaps the answer was that because almost all the officers of the 108th would undoubtedly be eager to transfer to the 118th, and because most of the men would, in the finest army tradition, follow their officers even to the cannon's mouth, there wouldn't be any 108th left.

While this unstructured chatter had been going on, one imperious-looking gentleman with a broad forehead and neat beard that gave him more than a passing resemblance to Edward VII had been making himself conspicuous by glowering silently. This was S.J. (Sam) Williams, president of Williams, Greene & Rome Co., who manufactured shirts with the help of 600 employees in three factories. He had been born in Indiana some 60 years earlier and had set up shop in Berlin in 1886. Though he had been president of the Board of Trade in 1900-1901, he was not much interested in public office or anything that would take him away from his shirts. His métier was lobbying in back rooms, or issuing fiats for others to pursue. When Cleghorn finally asked him if he had an opinion that he would like to express, he was blunt and to the point. "I am strongly opposed to calling a meeting for a purpose like this in the way that this meeting has been called tonight," he said, and then went on to state authoritatively how it should be done. First of all you select your two or three most influential men and charge them with the responsibility of selecting 30 or so others who are noted for their energy and efficiency. This large committee is then divided into sub-committees for publicity, finance, entertainment, and so on, and there you have your organization for recruiting 1,100 men. It was all so simple, so lucid. No one could figure out why he hadn't thought of it himself. The group immediately set about selecting their "three most influential men." The first turned out to be (who else?) Sam Williams; the other two were McBrine and Lochead. This more or less brought the meeting to a happy conclusion, but before everyone departed, secure in the knowledge that a full battalion was now well on the way to being raised, Williams dampened their optimism with some grave words of warning. No, it was not going to be simple. Without organization and effort they would not be able to winkle out the necessary recruits due to "certain failings" in the population of the riding. Indeed, startling as it might sound, he had been reliably informed that there were people living not 10 miles from Berlin who didn't even know there was a war on. So never mind that Berlin had contributed more per capita to the Patriotic Fund than anywhere else in Canada, and never mind that some splendid chaps had plucked the Kaiser's bust from its pedestal and tossed into the lake. That was all a year ago, and there was a lot still to be proved. "If there's any place in Canada that cannot afford to fall down in the matter of recruiting for overseas service," he concluded, "it is North Waterloo." The comment needed no elaboration.

The next meeting was held two days later on Wednesday, November 10. Only 13 people, presumably selected by the three wise men, were invited, and their task was to refine the organizational blueprint of Monday night. Williams was happy for the chair to be taken by E.W. Clement of the well-known legal family, and the latter proposed that a powerful executive committee of five men be formed, each one to preside over five important sub-committees. A committee was formed right away to make specific proposals along these lines and bring them back to the committee of the whole. It was a nice example of When In Doubt Strike Committees.

But organization wasn't the only topic. There was also further discussion about the practical problems of recruiting, and once again Williams delivered himself of strong warnings. He emphasized that they would be foolish to think that a campaign that simply encouraged volunteering would have any success. More militant methods of persuasion would have to be employed. A census, for example, should be taken of every eligible young man in the district. Each one should be sent a letter, and if the letter was not acknowledged it should be followed up by a visit from a member of the committee (a Visiting Sub-Committee?) who would "put the question strongly." Young men should be accosted in the streets and asked why they weren't in uniform. The "fair sex" shoud be invited to use their charms on the reluctant and their powers of persuasion on the recalcitrant. It all sounded very fair in theory; no one foresaw how nasty it would become in practice. Another part of the discussion was devoted to tentative quotas. Berlin itself, it was felt, should aim for about 500 recruits. Waterloo had earlier set its target at 227 men, which meant that it was undertaking to raise one of the four companies (C Company) that would constitute the battalion. The balance would come from the surrounding countryside which, of course, was sprinkled with villages bearing such unpromising names as Heidelberg, New Hamburg, Mannheim, Bamberg, Breslau, and Baden.

Williams had one further piece of business. He had just received a letter from Hamilton announcing a recruiting conference for all the recruiting leagues in the central and western parts of the province, to be held that Friday in the officer's mess of the 91st Regiment at the Hamilton Armouries. Every other major centre was going through the same exercise as Berlin at this time, and to pool ideas and experiences was only sensible. The Hamilton recruiters even appended a possible agenda, from which it could be gathered that they were as keen as mustard about the task ahead. Item five, for example, proposed that government employees who refused to enlist should be fired and that their jobs should be given to returning veterans; item seven suggested that recruiting sergeants be paid a fixed sum for each recruit they brought in—a type of piece work presumably, and one that was redolent of the good old days of the press gang. The Berliners thought it all sounded very promising, enthusiastically accepted the invitation, and promptly formed a Selection Committee to choose a Hamilton Committee to represent the riding.

Altogether 21 people from Berlin and Waterloo drove down on Friday morning, and this was proudly claimed to be the largest delegation from any centre apart from the host city. Nothing much came out of the conference, but then probably nothing much was expected. It was more like a convention, where the essential purpose is not so much to exchange useful information as to offer mutual congratulations and moral encouragement. The Berlin *Telegraph* thought that it was an excellent conference, but devoted as much of its report to the enjoyable luncheon at the Wentworth Arms and the laudatory speeches that followed as to anything else. Resolutions were, of course, passed, and a Provincial Executive of Recruiting Leagues (or PERL as it would have been called today) was formed. Williams was the Berlin representative, but he may have realized that such a provincial body had no real part to play in the basic task of putting a human being into a khaki uniform. As has been suggested, the cold fact of the matter was that the recruiting business was first and last a local undertaking, and its success depended solely on local energies and initiatives. Indeed, the conference may have had an unforeseen negative effect as far as North Waterloo was concerned. The setting up of links between cities meant that the aspirations, promises, quotas, and successes of each became more visible. An element of competition crept in. And as the weeks passed, and poor Berlin was seen to be better at producing large delegations than troops, the pressure to increase the numbers of the latter was heightened by a sensitivity to how well the others were doing and what others might be thinking of them. The inevitable result was civic embarrassment, which turned to frustration and then to bitterness and anger.

The final step in the mustering of the riding to arms came with the realization that if the whole district was to be effectively covered, the organizational tentacles would have to reach out into the country towns. The orderly Clement suggested an extension of the committee solution. Each town—Elmira, Linwood, Baden, Wellesley, and so on—would create its own sub-committees matching those in Berlin, and their chairmen would make up the central sub-committees. In order to put this plan into effect, a general meeting of the whole of North Waterloo was arranged for Friday, November 19, at 7:45 p.m. in the Berlin city hall, and foraging parties (they were actually called committees) were sent out to each of the outlying towns to invite representatives to attend. Each automobile was to be accompanied by an officer in uniform to add that extra touch of military swagger. Thus, on Wednesday, Colonel Lochead motored in the Cleghorn committee car to Elmira, and Captain Lockhart went with the A.R. Lang committee to Wellesley.

Within two and a half weeks, then, the blueprint for a web of committees covering the whole riding had been established, and the centralized Citizens' Recruiting Committee of North Waterloo was about to be formed. The inaugural Friday night meeting was a great success. According to the *News-Record,*

> there were present military men, business men, manufacturers, professional men and working men, and the addresses given and the enthusiasm displayed could not do otherwise than give an impetus to the movement towards raising a battalion from the district, with the co-operation of North Wellington which will handle its own organization work.

The first order of business was the election of officers. There could only be one candidate for president, the title that bestows laurels without labour, and Williams was duly honoured. His vice-president was W.G. Weichel, M.P. McBrine was chairman, though later he seems once again to have asked Cleghorn to take over the job, and DeBus, the ubiquitous barber who involved himself in as many issues as he could, became secretary. There were five committees, Publicity, Recruiting, Finance and Insurance, Transportation, and Press. The Publicity Committee was composed of J.F. Honsberger, one of Berlin's most influential and respected doctors, C.H. Mills, the Conservative M.P.P., Lochead, Weichel, and Williams. Recruiting was in the hands of Clement, E.H. Scully, brother of the city auditor, and H.J. Sims, the city solicitor. DeBus also managed to get onto this committee. W.E. Gallagher, another important player in the events of the next year, was on the Finance and Insurance Committee. He was a printer on the *Telegraph,* a former president of the Twin Cities Trades and Labour Council, and seems to have been the only "working man" involved at this stage. He was also an alderman and had come first in the polls in the 1915 election. On the Press Committee were the editors, and deadly rivals, of the two daily papers, and also Fred Krug, the jovial superintendent of the Arnott Institute for Stammerers and Stutterers, and O. Rumpel, who was in felt and boots.

As well as a slate of officers, a constitution was also adopted. This included the terms of reference for each committee. For example, "The Recruiting Committee shall prepare a list of all men eligible for military service with particulars as to age, whether married or single, occupation, responsibilities, if any, interfering with enlistment, and any other information which will be of use to the Recruiting Authorities." The meeting was also informed that because expert military opinion held that allowing recruits to board at home was not conducive to discipline, the toughening-up process and general gung-hoery, a central barracks had been sought, and that Williams had generously offered one of his empty W.G. & R. Co. premises at a rental of $10 per 1,000 square feet. The work of converting this factory, at the corner of Courtland and Queen, into a barracks, and the house next door into officers' quarters was to proceed right away.

Finally, there were some initial reports about what might be expected from the outlying districts. Apparently the Linwood area (pop. 550) looked promising and was expected to supply about 20 men, but the prospects in Wellesley (pop. 500) were not so bright. Williams, who seems to have had a nose for potential trouble spots, insisted that he had been told that "quite a number" of young Mennonites were likely to answer the call, though he didn't identify the author of this remarkable piece of optimism. It was left to the M.P. for the riding to give clear expression to the worry that still lay like a submerged log in everyone's mind. "It is time," said Weichel, "for a man to be a man, and to be a good Canadian citizen one must be a Britisher. I feel sure that the people of German extraction here realize and appreciate the benefits they enjoy, and I have no fear that North Waterloo will supply its full quota." And so the meeting concluded. Everything was off to a fine start. Indeed, in the preceeding few days 50 men had already enrolled in the 118th, and now that the North Waterloo Recruiting League was fully operational it surely wouldn't take long to fill the battalion.

This optimism was given a fillip the following week when it was learnt that Lt. Colonel Martin of the 71st Battalion, Galt, had been granted permission by Ottawa to transfer to the 118th, and that as many of the men in his company as wished to follow him might do so. (The 71st had been formed before the 118th and as a consequence contained a number of Berliners.) Colonel Martin, a popular officer, made the announcement to his men on the parade ground. As he said with the greatest sincerity, "I have absolutely no intention of influencing anyone, but all those men who wish to accompany me take one step forwards." All 132 men did so. No one analyzed the psychology of the moment, but Berlin was delighted and Galt was furious. So furious that the instructions were read more carefully, and it was found that only those who actually came from North Waterloo were allowed to transfer. This was initially said to cut the number back to 80. In the final event, 64 made the short trip north — only half what the earliest rumours promised, but in the recruiting stakes you took them where you found them, even if this meant poaching in neighbouring woods. Anyway, 64 more than doubled the battalion's strength at a blow, and this clearly called for a civic celebration.

The new recruits arrived on Saturday evening, November 27, and were given what the *Telegraph* called "a rousing welcome," but the phrase may have been more formulaic than accurate. The *News-Record*, in an ingenious piece of rhymed reportage, gives a different impression:

> I've almost come to think for sure that we're a lot of blokes —
> that we poor simperin' Berliners be a horrid lot of jokes. Why,
> bless my boots, we stood about, several thousand strong — we
> surely made a spectacle, a line some distance long. We went to
> see the soldiers come, they'd come not many miles, but
> reckoned they'd be greeted with a thousand cheers and smiles.
> But, say, we stood in rows just like the taters on the hills, or like
> a load of beans and oats bein' carted to the mills. We have the
> lungs, you bet we have, when hockey games are on; oh, then
> our lungs and speaking pipes are most alarmin' strong. But
> when the troops come marchin' in, to spend the winter here, we
> seem to be ascared to death to hoot one little cheer. Oh, shucks,
> let's tear things loose some time, and make sure we aren't dead,
> and show that we've a shoutin' mouth stuck crossways in our
> head. Gee whiz, let's pinch our skinny bones to see if we're
> alive, and next time that we see the troops, blow up and let her
> drive.

It was, then, a curious and somewhat silent crowd that lined the route as the ex-Galt contingent marched from the car barns at Albert and King to city hall. But this was only the first part of the gauntlet they had to run. Next were the speeches. At city hall they were drawn up in ranks and, while the night got darker and a sharpish wind gusted down from the north-west, they were welcomed first by Mayor Hett, then by Cleghorn, then by Lochead, then by Martin, and finally by the indefatigable Williams, who had somewhere stumbled across the foul rumour, apparently upsetting many mothers, that certain unnatural practices were rife in barracks life. "There is less chance of a boy losing his self-respect in the army than out," he thundered, while 64 faces gently froze in the November gloom. Finally it was all over, and they were marched back to the Berlin Restaurant where they were treated to supper by the I.O.D.E. For lads on their way to the trenches it was all no doubt excellent basic training in the development of the philosophic mind.

The night before had witnessed another gala event; the district's first bumper recruiting rally. It was held in the Waterloo town hall, and as the main speakers the Publicity Committee had procured the services of Toronto's own Mrs. Willoughby Cummings, whose very name conjures up images of Union Jacks snapping in the breeze, and the Reverend W.A. Cameron of the Bloor Street Baptist Church, who seems to have been something of a fixture on the war-effort talk circuit. The hall, strung with streamers and flags, was packed full; there was standing room only in the aisles; even the corridors outside were crowded. And up at the front of this military revival meeting the recruiting sergeants were at their desks, ready to accept the pledges of those who came forward to make their decision for King and Country.

An excerpt from Cameron's speech is worth quoting because it gives the flavour of the rhetoric of what one might call the innocent, early days of Berlin's recruiting campaign. The tone now is lofty, inspirational, even visionary; when the intransigence of the population becomes clearer, it becomes more abrasive and derisory.

> I come to you to speak on the challenges of war. In the first place there is the challenge of the past; of those from your country, and others, who have given their lives in the good cause. They are the kings of humanity; all hearts are their empire. I know that after the war you will appreciate more than now that these are the heroes, and that this is the pathway to glory.

Then there is the spirit of those who have answered the last roll call, the soldiers who have gone beyond, and the Edith Cavells of Flanders and Belgium who have suffered and died. Can any man with a heart in him at all fail his country beneath a heaven starred with the spirits of these men and women who have given their all for the cause?

There is the challenge of the men enduring for you in the trenches. If the response is quick, this endurance will not be as long as it otherwise would. But Britain will be on the battlefield as long as the other fellow. She will be there until the last day. Yes, she will be there a day longer. (Cheers)

Men, at the battle of Waterloo the men of Wellington who stood fast in that famous hollow square had their pipers to encourage them as they waited. The men at the front are listening today. The sound which will help them to endure the hardships of the battle line is the steady tramp of the advancing hosts of their comrades from all parts of the Empire. Let us hearten them with the cry, "We are coming General Kitchener! 500,000 strong!" (Prolonged cheers)

The modern tendency, prompted by an undemanding iconoclasm, is to wonder at the naivety of the millions who swallowed this sort of thing hook, line, and mustard gas. But perhaps we are in our own way just as gullible today—or perhaps even more gullible, as the cheap seductions of television (to take one small example) might suggest. Although the cause was misconceived and hugely tragic, at least Cameron was flirting with the heroic.

Two more recruiting rallies were held in December. The first, on Tuesday, December 7, was a double-barrelled affair that went off simultaneously at the town hall in Waterloo and the Grand Theatre in Berlin. The speakers, who swapped places during the evening, were the Honourable Martin Burrell, Minister of Agriculture, the Reverend F.M. Wooten of Galt, who brought the traditional divine approval, and Lt. Forneret, a veteran recuperating from wounds but itching to get back to the Front for another crack at the *Bosche*. All three speakers made a point of acknowledging the Germanness of North Waterloo, but urged the necessity of rising above remote and threadbare ties in the face of the threat to democracy. Two days later, at the Star Theatre, it was the turn of provincial ministers F.G. McDiarmid (Public Works) and T.W. McGarry (Treasurer) to inspire the youth of Berlin. Unfortunately they only managed to inspire one youth between the two of them. This represented a 100 percent drop from the previous meeting.

Meanwhile, the outlying villages were also being blitzed with mini-rallies, the speakers on these occasions being the tireless members of the Recruiting League—Elmira on November 30, Wellesley on December 8, Linwood on December 9, Conestogo on December 10, Hawkesville and Crosshill on December 13, and St. Clements and Heidelberg on December 15. Each of these meetings followed a format similar to those of the bigger entertainments in town. First of all the flag and uniform would be displayed as prominently as possible (at the Grand Theatre meeting of December 7 the highlight, which brought the wildly cheering audience to its feet, was the arrival of the 118th, preceded by its bugle band), and then there would be two or three main speakers whose homilies would be alternated with vaudeville numbers of a comic or patriotic nature. Both in and out of town, the Dominion Tire Quartette figured prominently, with such numbers as "We'll Never Let The Old Flag Fall" and "The Girl Who Is Yours While You Are Away," both said to be great hits in Toronto; while Douglas McKaye, billed as "Dominion Tire Co.'s Harry Lauder," supplied the Highland humour. And when the resources of Dominion Tire were exhausted there was always Miss Ida Dunke, soprano, and Fred Krug, piano, to offer such rousers as "The King Will Be Proud Of Canada."

The most successful piece of recruiting seems to have taken place at Elmira where, after the November 30 rally, a soldier was left behind to drum up business. This was the famous Company Sergeant Major Granville Blood. Though still quite a young man at the beginning of the war, Blood had already served in the Royal Navy, and it was due to this experience that he quickly became the senior N.C.O. of A Company. One eyewitness describes him as a handsome, tough, six-footer, and a contemporary photograph, taken either at London or Camp Borden, supports the evidence that he was a man of confident authority—though there is also the suggestion that some of his 'weight' may have resided in his waist. This, however, may be due to the bulky wool uniform he is wearing. He was a fearless and fearsome leader of men, and also rabidly patriotic, though one source alleges that it was his wife, Agnes, who was the real power behind this particular throne and that it was she who pushed him into some of his more outrageous exploits. Whatever the truth of the matter, Blood was to play as central a role in this story as anyone. On this, his first appearance, we find him returning to Berlin with 10 young Elmirans in tow. In the light of his subsequent escapades, one wonders what his methods of conscription were.

Needless to say, rallies and parades were not the only tactics employed by the Recruiting League. Considerable efforts were also made to publicize the comforts of army life. Early in December, for example, it was agreed that a Khaki Club should be founded to look after the social and recreational needs of the lads. The premises were again obtained by Williams, who was most helpful when it came to moving a couple out of their flat before their lease had expired so that the Club could become a reality as soon as possible. Donations of furniture and equipment for this home away from home began to flow in with encouraging speed. There was also to be free use of the St. Jerome's swimming pool. What more could a boisterous young man ask for! Well, one answer would be a nice place to live, and here again the highest expectations were realized. Indeed, if newspaper accounts are anything to go by, the metamorphosis of the W.G. & R. factory that had been going on for the past month was as miraculous and beautiful as the emergence of a butterfly from its cocoon. As the *News-Record* described it, it was the very Royal York of barracks, the finest in the Dominion. The nine gleaming gas stoves in the kitchen, the cosy bunks for 700 men, the spotless white table stretching the length of the mess, all were described in bated prose. As for cleanliness being next to pugnacity, "after an inspection of the orderly room the ablution room is the next room to surprise the visitor. This is fitted out with galvanized iron washstands and fourteen shower baths. To the left of the ablution room is the toilet room sanitarily equipped with automatic flushers working every two minutes." Obviously any able-bodied young man who didn't rush right on down to take the shilling (or, more, precisely, $1.10 *per diem*), and thereby take advantage of this salubrious palace needed his head examined.

Unfortunately, an awful lot of young heads needed examining. In spite of all the speeches, in spite of all the bedecked cars criss-crossing the riding in search of warlike lads, in spite of all the songs and bugles and bunting, the recruits only dribbled and drabbled in, when what was needed was a good, strong flow. At the Christmas dinner at the barracks on December 29, 1915, only about 200 men sat down to enjoy the 200 lbs. of goose and 60 lbs. of plum pudding (the latter courtesy of the ladies of Berlin) and that simply wasn't good enough, particularly when one remembered that a third of that number had been a windfall from Galt. Sam Hughes had been promised 1,100 men by Spring, but if getting the first 100 or so into khaki had been as tough as pulling teeth, then how or where on North Waterloo earth were another 900 to be acquired? The populace had been cajoled, tempted, exhorted, flattered, praised, reassured, and made indignant in ways both great and small. What more could be done? Perhaps little stories such as the one reprinted from the *Hamilton Times* to the effect that Germany had coloured Canada green in its new atlases to indicate that it was going to be a Prussian colony after the war might summon up some indignant blood. Or a snippet from the *Goderich Signal* maintaining that "the khaki uniform is much more becoming than the red tunic, and it improves almost any man's appearance. It is said the khaki colour suits every man's complexion unless he is yellow." Surely that fashion note would persuade all but the hopelessly jaundiced. The real culprits, of course, were the young, unattached males, of whom there were known to be plenty around. Statistics were already beginning to turn up the interesting fact that as many married men were enlisting as single men, and that, as the *News-Record* sternly said, did not say much for single men. There was no suggestion that it might have said even less for marriage.

Other items of news only served to heighten the tension. At the end of the year Canada raised its commitment to 300,000 men. Closer to home, the news from Galt was that their battalion would soon be oversubscribed in spite of the depletion mentioned earlier. What was the matter with Berlin, Ontario? As the spectre of failure, of community humiliation, slowly loomed, the composure of the recruiters receded. Patience began to give way to panic, and courtesy to loutishness. In December of 1915 these changes of attitude were undramatic, but they were evident nevertheless. The search for scapegoats was, of course, one of the inevitable consequences of the recruiting failure, and from the start the finger was pointed at internal subversion. Publications sympathetic to Germany were said to be coming across the border from the United States and being sold on city newsstands. Furthermore, some churches (one remembers that half of them were still entirely German-speaking) and church magazines were accused of openly espousing the enemy cause. At the Recruiting League meeting of December 11, Dr. Honsberger unequivocally charged the Benton Street Baptist Church with being a major offender in this regard. Adding fuel to this fear of the enemy within were the stories, which began to increase in number from now on, of enemy saboteurs. On December 23, attempted sabotage was suspected in a Hamilton munitions factory, and the possible plot was traced back to Berlin. On the same date, two men called Koenig and Leyendicker were indicted in the United States for conspiring to dynamite the Welland Canal.

But it was on the front line of recruiting, as it were, that the more dramatic changes began to take place in Berlin. The troops themselves, imbued with the swagger of heroes — after all, they had already displayed their manhood by enlisting — quickly and correctly assessed all the hot air emanating from the clerics and politicians and plutocrats as not worth a cent, if for no other reason than that potential recruits knew better than to attend the rallies. All the shouting and the cheers and the "tigers" rose from middle-aged and geriatric throats. The real market, in other words, was not even being reached because it lurked furtively in billiard parlours, or ethnic clubs with questionable allegiances, or skulked behind its mothers' apron strings. If this was the case, then Mahomet would have to go to the mountain, and the troops would carry him there. This campaign started off innocuously enough, with packs of soldiers roaming the streets and shouting names such as "Yellowback!" at likely looking wardodgers. Not the most effective psychology, perhaps, but there was an improvement when the battalion officers began to organize this rather haphazard civilian baiting. Now, when a possible victim was sighted, 20 or 30 men would surround him, and after a spot of verbal horseplay, an officer would enter the ring and give the presumably somewhat nervous recruit a personalized recruiting speech. After this he would be "escorted" to the recruiting office, where he would come face to face with the formidable Sgt. Major Blood. No assault, no battery (not yet anyway). Just friendly persuasion. Or, as the *Telegraph*, which thoroughly approved of these sidewalk capers, explained it, "They do not force him to enlist, but they force him to hear why he should enlist."

A variation of this tactic was employed on Monday, December 13, when Captain Kreitzer and about 60 men went on night manoeuvres. The objective was the city's clubs and pool halls where, as everyone knew, a good percentage of those who should be learning how to hate the "Hun" were chalking cue tips, sipping beer, and quite probably singing *Deutschland über Alles*. The first place to be hit was the Royal Billiard Parlour at 36 King Street East, just down from the American Hotel. The men burst in, locked the doors, and then the dashing Captain Kreitzer leapt up onto a pool table and harangued the astounded players. From here it was up around the corner to the Lutheran Club on Frederick, where the same general performance was repeated, and finally to the Lyric Club. This establishment, however, had been tipped off by some mute, inglorious Paul Revere, so that when the soldiers arrived they found the doors barricaded. Unfortunately, the transoms had been left open, and a scaling party soon effected an entry and opened the gates to the main army. After the clubs the men, now in the greatest high spirits, took to the streets and hustled 20 able-bodied men to the recruiting office, where withering scorn was poured upon their pitiful excuses. One pacifist, who was asked the classic trick question about what he'd do if he saw his mother being molested by a *Bosche*, considered for a moment and then replied that he'd want to know the circumstances first—a reply almost as singular as that of Huxley who, when asked the same question, replied that he'd try to get in between them.

This Monday night escapade, although it appears to have netted nine recruits, was probably going a little too far a little too soon as far as public acceptability was concerned. Anyway, it wasn't immediately repeated. It is even possible that some aspects of it could come under the heading of "boyish pranks." No one was actually hurt, and no premises were wrecked. That was to come later. But it is also true that as 1915 drew to a close the strain was beginning to tell in Busy Berlin. Perhaps a silly little incident that occurred towards the end of the month conveys the flavour best. John Schaefer, a farmer on the Petersburg Road, came driving up behind the 118th as it was marching along Queen Street South. It was not the first time that Schaefer and the army had met like this, but on this occasion it resulted in a court case. The column was marching in three companies, four men abreast. They overlapped the centre line, but there was still "plenty of room for the motor to pass." However, Schaefer was said to have suddenly swung out from the rear of the column in order to overtake it, "nearly" striking Captain Pratt, and actually hitting Private Vasiloff when he got to the middle of the column. He then turned sharply into the head of the column. Schaefer, of course, denied these allegations with the somewhat belligerent statement, "If I'd wanted to hit them I'd have started at the back and run right through them!" and he laughed at the charge that Vasiloff had been hit. However, it is hard for one man to contradict 125 witnesses, and Magistrate Weir fined him $20 and costs. It all sounds very much like one of those episodes that starts as a shoving match and ends as a fist fight. It is quite possible that Schaefer had taken to buzzing the column every time he met it on his way to town, and that he eventually provoked retaliation. It is equally possible that Vasiloff did a stumbling act in order to ingratiate himself with his commanding officer; or was even told to do so. Wherever the truth lies, it is apparent that by the end of the year battlelines were being drawn in Berlin, and the causes of them were becoming clearer. As one newspaper acknowledged, "The soldiers do not call the civilians friends any more." And the civilians for their part were not by any means going to be cowed into silence, let alone into the ranks of the 118th Battalion. Not all civilians of course. Some were vociferous supporters of the soldiers and encouraged them in every possible way. The majority, however, held their peace and were troubled.

THREE

Soldiers versus Citizens

In Berlin, Ontario, the New Year began full of promise. The weather was mild, the economy was booming, and C.S.M. Blood, when asked for his New Year's resolution, got it mixed up with birthdays and wished for lots more men to go with him to France. Those who had already joined the 118th had had a restful holiday season. Some had gone home on leave, and the rest had been spared the route marches and square-bashing that were the usual regimen for troops in training for the Flanders mud — though in Berlin it was more grass than square-bashing, as their drill ground was Victoria Park, where they would form fours and wheel in column of route under the watchful eye of Queen Victoria and small boys in knickerbockers and cloth caps.

And there were other signs that army life was not to be without a reasonable amount of beer, if not skittles. George "Pop" Phillips, the legendary manager of the Roma Theatre, made Thursday night free for the boys of the 118th, and no doubt many of them took advantage of the privilege at the beginning of the year to see Ethel Barrymore in the five-act photo drama, *The Final Judgement*. On January 4, the spanking new Khaki Club was finally ready for business on the second and third floors of the old Auditorium on Queen Street South. Here the recruits could shoot some pool or play checkers and chess, write letters, read magazines, or if they wanted something more physical, they could go on up to the third floor and work out in the gym with its horizontal bars, rowing machines, and punching bags. All splendid training for dealing with the "Hun," whether at home or abroad. The gym could also convert into a concert hall for regular Monday night "smokers" at which the battalion's talent could show off its paces. Private McCumber, for example, was famous for his clog dances, and it wasn't unusual for Sgt. Major Blood to belt out "The Road To Mandalay" as a finale.

The Khaki Club was supervised by Fred Coyne of the Y.M.C.A. He had his office at the top of the first flight of stairs, and from here he orchestrated the innumerable dinners that every church group in the city wanted to lay on for the lads, arranged lectures of an improving nature on such topics as "Christ In The Holy Land" and "A Trip Through The Picturesque Rockies," and set up French classes which, of course, would come in particularly handy when the battalion got to Europe. In other words, he was charged with the spiritual and physical welfare of the young men living away from home for the first time. The appointment was probably as much tactical as humanitarian. Parental opposition was often cited as an explanation why young men were not coming forward in the expected droves, and one reason for this opposition was the rumour, so angrily denounced by Sam Williams, that unhealthy practices were not unknown in an army barracks. What better way to allay these fears than have a member of the Y.M.C.A. to keep an eye on things.

Another event that momentarily helped to deflect attention from grimmer civic issues was the arrival on Friday, January 7, of a contingent of Australian cadets, now nearing the end of a year-long tour of the continent. The citizens, or at least those not beavering away on the factory floors for the war effort, flocked to the Grand Trunk Railway (G.T.R.) station on Victoria to greet these exotic visitors from Down Under when their train pulled in at 10:05 a.m. According to the *News-Record*, which reported their stay in some detail, everyone seems to have been enchanted by the 36 handsome teenagers in their neat blue uniforms who leapt smartly out of the train and formed up behind their marching band. Accompanied by an honour guard from the 118th, the Khaki Club Committee, the City Council, and a crowd of citizenry, they swung jauntily down Water Street, wheeled left onto King, and marched through the centre of town to city hall, where Mayor Hett gave them a predictable Busy Berlin welcome. "I trust that you will find many interesting sights in our industrial city," he said. "It has more than one hundred and twenty five manufacturing establishments, many of which you will visit this afternoon." One suspects a collective spasm in young Aussie limbs, but Lt. Simons, their commander, quickly called on them to give the curious crowd their exuberant Kangaroo Cheer. "Aus-Aus-Australia! Cooee! Cooee! Cooee!

Berlin!" screamed the cadets, with appropriate physical gyra-
tions. Berlin was captivated, and for the rest of the day the
"Cooees!" rang out all over the city.

The visitors' agenda for the day was daunting, though no
doubt a repetition of what they had experienced in every city in
Canada and the States in which they'd stopped over the past
year. First there were visits to the city's schools to meet their
peer groups. Then they were introduced to the wealthy Berliners
who had agreed to billet them, the Langs, the Krugs, the Rum-
pels, the Breithaupts, the McBrines. At 5:30 there was a banquet
at the Canadian Club, and at 8:15 they performed their own
patriotic entertainment, *Called To The Front*, at the Grand. They
did, however, get one break. Some subversive spirit booked the
ice rink for them for the afternoon, and when they were given
the option of skating or the dreaded educational tours of factories, they chose the former. This puzzled some Berliners. Why
would anyone want to spend the afternoon skating about on his
ankles, as Australians would tend to do, when he could watch
rubber footwear being made. Still, boys will be boys, especially
Australians.

The evening's banquet sealed the popularity of the visitors.
Canada's most memorable feature, said Lt. Simons in his speech
of thanks, is its pies.

> Someone once said, "The sun never sets on the British Empire."
> Of this I am sure, it never sets on Canada without throwing a
> shadow over a pie. (Loud laughter) In Canada I believe you
> could walk from Halifax to Vancouver on them. We have had so
> many we will remember them all our lives.

It is not known whether Lt. Simons was being ironical about
Canadian pies, but certainly another cultural feature that he
mentioned remains unchanged.

> We in Australia had heard of the keen, invigorating atmosphere
> enjoyed by Canadians, but upon arrival here we find you apply-
> ing everything that human ingenuity can devise to keep it out of
> your homes. Outside you freeze your ears, and inside you have
> to suck a piece of ice to keep cool. I believe that when Cana-
> dians get into the next world there will be a terrible run on Cay-
> enne pepper. (Prolonged applause)

But the speech wasn't all jokes. Lt. Simons had been well
briefed about the tensions that would shortly tear the community apart, and if he took a Polyanna approach to them, that was
only fitting for an ambassador of goodwill. "Here in Berlin you

have the offspring of two different races living in perfect harmony. In Southern Australia, as in Berlin, we have German settlements and in the present crisis their adhesion to Empire is as strong and loyal as those of any other part of the Commonwealth." There were, of course, limits even to Lt. Simons's wishful thinking about racial tolerance. Australia is, as he firmly pointed out, within a few days' sail of "ambitious orientals," and there was no question that his was to be "a white man's country; a country with one heart, one idea, one colour, one language, and one government." The patriotism of one age is the racism of the next. But though such matters are in a constant state of flux, at least Love remains the same. The next morning at the station the dashing cadets were surrounded by a mob of young girls, some with their handkerchiefs out, who pressed on them mementos and addresses. One wonders how so many hearts could be broken in such a short time, but then Australians were always fast workers. Now the tour was to move on. Two days before it had been Brantford. Today the Kangaroo Cheer would be heard in Guelph. Soon they would all be home again. Then, for some, there would be death in Europe.

The departure of the Australians brought the holiday season to an end in more ways than one. Now the tricky business of getting 800 or 900 local men into uniform had to be very firmly addressed if civic shame was to be avoided. The splendid recruiting results in Galt were already well known; Stratford and London were reporting similar successes. By comparison Berlin was pathetic. And everyone knew why. It was the enemy in our midst. Well, the enemy would simply have to be isolated, grappled with, and generally attacked on all fronts—morally, emotionally, spiritually—and, if necessary, physically.

One method of getting the message across, basically used in every city, was through newspaper advertisements. These appealed not only to the patriotic sentiments of eligible young men, but to others with vested interests as well. To mothers, for example. "HAVE YOU MOTHERED A MAN?" thundered one full-page advertisement in the *News-Record*. "SOME WOMEN HAVE GIVEN MANY SONS TO THE COUNTRY'S CAUSE, SOME WOMEN (WHO CAN) HAVE NOT GIVEN ONE." An equally shrill message was directed at sweethearts and girlfriends.

> BAR THEM OUT YOU WOMEN. Refuse their invitations, scorn their attentions. For the love of Heaven, if they wont be men, then you be women. Show that you despise him. Get the apologist, the weakling, the mother's pet, into the service. Weed out

all and we will find out who are the cowards. Analyze your friends, you women, refuse their attentions and tell them why. Make them wake up. God Bless Him. The King Calls.

But where this advertisement descends into gibberish, other appeals were more nicely targetted. One was addressed to hockey players, and in particular, one assumes, to the team goon (or "policeman" as the modern euphemism has it). "Hockey players — attention! Listen to what the president of the O.H.A says: — Exchange the puck and stick for the Ross rifle and bayonet and take your place in the great army that is being formed to sweep the oppressors of humanity from the face of the earth." With hockey stick or Ross rifle (and it was arguable as to which was the more effective weapon) the goon was a prized commodity. And for those of a more spiritual bent there was always the likes of Father J.J. O'Gorman of Ottawa to put the fear of God into the chicken-hearted. "For a young man to shirk what is evident to him as his manifest duty, and through selfishness refuse to enlist, IS UNDOUBTEDLY A SIN." The fact that the majority of churchgoers in Berlin were German-speaking Lutherans (and most of the Roman Catholics were also German-speaking) may have meant that the Reverend Father's malediction lacked bite.

And so it went on. Day after day, advertisements in every single issue of both papers directed their call to arms to every possible constituency, but to all intents and purposes the efforts were both practically useless and psychologically unsatisfying. One didn't know who read the newspapers. One didn't know whether the message was getting through. It was like firing random bursts into a jungle in the hopes of hitting an invisible enemy. Except that the annoying thing was that the enemy wasn't all that invisible. He could be seen every night on King Street, swanning about with his hands in his pockets. How one would like to put the bastards up against the wall (very gently to be sure) and ask them a question or two! Or frog march them down to the recruiting office (oh so politely) and give them a spot of the Sergeant Bloods. Eight hundred men were still needed. Time was getting short. The street-recruiting methods of the previous month must be brought back, but this time with a little more aggression.

As we have seen, the streets were only one of the places to hunt the "Yellowback," and perhaps not the best one, because although some were incredibly brazen about parading their cowardice, others were wary of open spaces. Kreitzer's pre-

Christmas experiments had shown that it was sometimes productive to track them into their haunts of entertainment, and for a time this *modus operandi* was continued. For example, one evening early in January, the Captain and his merry men went on safari once again. This time they tried Gettas and Gettas, the popular family restaurant on King Street (cakes and ices a specialty). Here a party of young people were enjoying their dinner in a private room, when in strode the Captain and began to harangue them over their entrées. "Enjoying our meal, are we? Everyone comfortable? A lot more comfortable I bet than our boys in the trenches! What I suggest to you young men is that you escort these fair ladies home, and then come on down to the recruiting office! Ladies, you should only entertain these physically fit young men when they're in khaki!" — or something like that, while the young men sheepishly kneaded their bread rolls. The ladies, however, were said to have been delighted and gave the gallant Captain a round of applause. What happened next is unrecorded, but it probably put a damper on the evening.

A week earlier, Captain McNeel had shown equal initiative when he delivered a recruiting speech during the intermission of *The Slender Maid*, a local amateur group's musical comedy, at the Grand Theatre. Unfortunately, there was a blizzard that night and the audience was sparse; but as is often the case with amateur theatricals, the cast was enormous (over 70 in this case), so the Captain's exhortations could be directed to both sides of the footlights. Nor did the message fall on stony ground. Doug McKaye, the male lead, accepted the challenge to exchange his theatrical costume for khaki, as did Fred Mullins, who played Tony, "a dago fruit vendor" and whose solo "Banana Ripe" had brought the house down. It was just bad luck for McNeel and the 118th that McKaye decided to enlist in Guelph and Mullins in London.

The other ranks were not to be outdone by their officers when it came to exploring new recruiting territory. The night after Captain Kreitzer's restaurant campaign, a group of them were watching *The Romance of Elaine* at the Roma Theatre, when they decided that there were too many young men in civvies in the audience. A spirited dialogue began, no doubt punctuated by cries of "Shut up!" and "Sit down!" and the like, which in turn led to a small-scale uproar and the intervention of Beckerich, the manager, who roundly berated the military for their unseemly conduct. The next night the soldiers, their numbers somewhat swollen, milled around outside the theatre, jostling people and shouting that the movies at the other theatres were a whole lot better and that everyone should go there instead. Beckerich complained to Colonel Lochead, but was informed that they were only loyal lads doing their duty for King and Country.

The bellicose approach was not the only one tried. Kreitzer also experimented with The Heart-rending Tale when, his voice breaking with emotion, he told the *News-Record* the melancholy story of Mrs. L. Cline of 365 Victoria Street, who appeared at the recruiting office one morning with her youngest son, Gordon, in tow. "Take him Captain," said the distraught mum (according to Kreitzer, who had clearly seen one too many lachrymose melo-dramas),

> he is my last and is all I have left to give. I don't want to part with him, Captain. He's the last of six. I do so want to keep him with me for he's not over strong, but he's so anxious to go that my poor heart can't refuse him. I'll be broken-hearted without him, but still I'm glad he wants to go. It's better for him to go with your battalion, Captain, as his brother is already with you. Arthur may be able to do so much for poor Gordon if they are together. I wish he could stay with me for I'll be all alone now. Captain, do I love my boys less than other mothers who wont let their boys go? Tell me Captain. My poor mother's heart is well nigh breaking, yet I must let him go. My last, my last, oh Captain, Captain!

On Monday, January 17, City Council made it official. The recruiting campaign wasn't working. The prickly Alderman Cleghorn proposed a motion, which passed unanimously, applauding all the efforts made to raise a battalion, but deploring the lack of patriotism in all and sundry. Alderman Master seconded the motion (and took a crack at the Turk; "if there are any two words that mean the same thing and that are spelled differently it is 'hell' and 'Turk'"), and Alderman Gallagher brought tears to the eyes of his fellow council members when he explained how much he wanted to enlist, but that he had a wife and three children to consider. No one was unkind enough to draw to his attention the statistics about the number of married as opposed to single recruits.

The anger of city hall acted as a catalyst on the soldiers. With such official backing surely they could stop pulling their punches on the streets, and maybe start throwing a few. It was all very well to make la-di-da speeches in restaurants and theatres; what some of these gutless creatures needed was a good thrashing. And thus it was that Saturday night, January 22, saw the first serious escalation of hostilities on the streets of Berlin. Fortified by alcohol, and clearly with the tacit approval of some officers, even encouraged, so rumour had it, by the promise of a dollar for every recruit signed up, they went on a rampage through the downtown area. Anything in trousers was fair game, and now it was no longer a matter of polite questions ("Excuse me, sir, but could you tell me why you're not in uniform?") or polite requests ("Would you mind coming down to the recruiting office for a few moments"), but of instant insults ("Why aren't you in− −uniform, you− −yellow belly?"−or words to that effect). Because violence inevitably breeds violence, the next statement was "Grab the− −," at which point six or seven soldiers set on the hapless civilian and carried or dragged him along the street to the recruiting office. Here he was deposited on the floor with torn clothes and bruised body, but at least now he was in the presence of officers, who were able to act as a restraining influence on their excited men− though even here one frenzied private had to be forcibly restrained when he tried to "get at" a particularly indignant civilian. As one officer privately admitted to the *News-Record*, "The action of some of those men was a damned disgrace. I believe if General Hughes knew about it he'd put the ban on it."

It was mainly on the downtown blocks of King Street that the muzzles came off and most of the action took place. Here the verbal abuse, described as "something fierce," and the physical assaults had little respect for age or sex. One couple, who had just come out of Gettas and Gettas after enjoying a family meal with their small daughter, were set upon by a group of soldiers led by an unnamed sergeant. Blood perhaps? The husband was grabbed. His wife screamed at them to leave him alone, but the sergeant bawled back, "You're one of those yellow ones are you!" The woman tried to explain that they were American citizens, but the sergeant ordered his men to hustle him off. Again the woman tried to intervene, but the sergeant roughly shoved her up against a wall. The woman hit him. The sergeant hit her back. The child had hysterics. And so the skirmishes went on through the evening, viewed, it may be noted, by the local constabulary, who maintained a token, though inconspicuous, presence. When one police officer was asked why he didn't put a stop to the lawlessness, he made the probably sane observation that to have tried to do so would have been to risk his life.

Of the many men hauled to the recruiting office that Saturday night, 12 were enlisted. Of these, five were later rejected as unfit. The total bag, then, for the night's work was seven men.

Berlin's reaction to this re-creation of nineteenth-century press-gang tactics was immediate. The *News-Record's* editorial, as ever, attempted to walk a thin, Solomon-like line between admonition and vindication. "Any measures which savour of compulsion are likely to defeat the object in view. Locally there may have been instances of over-zeal among some of those who have enlisted in their efforts to secure new members. If so, it can be put down to enthusiasm for the welfare of the battalion." The officers were interviewed, and from their defensive replies it is clear that they knew that matters had got out of hand — though of course it was by no means the fault of the soldiers. As Captain Fraser, the battalion adjutant put it, "the present methods, though degrading to a community and most grudgingly adopted by us, have been adopted only because our other methods have failed." Lt. Dingman was equally plaintive. The recruiting meetings were not being attended by the right sort of people, so what could the soldiers possibly do but resort to "strong personal appeals" or, to use Captain Routley's humbug, "a little gentle persuasion." And anyway, blustered Colonel Lochead with finality, "99% of the complaints when sifted have proved the blame rests with the civilians."

In spite of the rationalizations and the rhetoric and the armyspeak, Lochead was obviously so rattled by the public outcry that within 24 hours "Battalion Orders for Street Recruiting" had been issued to the men. These regulations, however, were so utterly absurd, so riddled with vaguely threatening provisos, that they did nothing to pacify the angry citizens. It is doubtful whether they were even legal. Point 4, for example, stated that "While it is permitted to address any man who appears fitted to don the Khaki, yet workers will not permit their zeal and enthusiasm to carry them away. Be firm and persuasive in your endeavours to induce men to enter the recruiting rooms . . . but do not resort to force unless circumstances absolutely warrant same." Point 5 reads: "No man is to be carried in or otherwise forced to come unless he (a) ignores proper questioning; (b) shows resentment; (c) or is insulting in his speech or action. Even when applying pressure no uncalled for roughness or horse-play of any kind is to be indulged in." There were enough loopholes here to drive a team of wild recruiting sergeants through them.

The most lucid reply to the "Battalion Orders" came from Charles Ruby, who was, interestingly enough, the Secretary of Mutual Life, Lochead's former (and future) company. Everyone, said Ruby, wants recruiting to be successful, and there's nothing wrong with a systematic, personal canvass, but at the same time it had to be remembered that "not only is a resort to force to compel men to enter the Recruiting Rooms a transgression of law for which the offenders ought to be prosecuted, but it is bound to defeat the object that is desired to be accomplished." He went on, "The officers of the 118th state 'we have always maintained that no citizen of apparent military age should resent the question — why are you not in khaki?' It seems to me that in the mandatory form in which the interrogation is made, it were strange if the question were *not* resented. It is a personal matter about which no man has the right to make a demand any more than he has the right to demand of another why he does not turn out his toes when he walks."

But if this was a measured and reasonable assessment of the recruiting situation (though Lochead was to mock his former business associate publicly the next day) other responses were not. On the Tuesday following Saturday night's debacle, the Twin City Trades and Labour Council passed a motion, fuelled by anger and dripping with contempt, in which after a series of "Whereases," which included references to the cost of housing soldiers in Berlin, to the amount of taxpayers' money already donated to patriotic causes, to "heroes" in uniform making themselves obnoxious in the sight of a freedom-loving people and to "several occasions of ladies being insulted," it was Resolved that Sam Hughes be requested to remove the battalion from Waterloo County if it didn't behave itself!

This frontal attack by the Council is a fascinating reminder that opposition to the war effort did not only divide along ethnic lines (indeed, it is probably true to say that a great many Berliners of whatever ethnic stripe were solidly in favour of raising a battalion in order to prove their loyalty to the rest of Canada); there were also the class divisions. At the same time as Berlin's civilians and soldiers were grappling on King Street, the Trades Union Congress in Britain was fighting hard against a conscription bill and thereby helping to move that country towards an election on this very issue. No doubt the workers of Berlin were well aware of what their brothers were up to across the Atlantic, and believed that their local skirmish with the military authorities was but a part of the great class struggle against what they

considered to be a capitalists' war. And not irrelevant to the
local spat was the fact that Lochead, the colonel of the embry-
onic battalion, was also the president of the Berlin Board of
Trade, a post, indeed, to which he was re-elected two days after
the Trades and Labour Council attack. As both Boss and Chief
Recruiter he could hardly have been a better target for the
workers' rage.

The *News-Record* informed Lochead of the Council's attack
and agreed to withhold publication of it so that he could write a
rebuttal to be published in the same issue. And a furious rebuttal it was, too. It was, said Lochead, "a scurulous (*sic*) resolution," and he proceeded to attack it clause by clause. The first
false statement, about the expense of providing quarters for the
battalion, he preferred to call "crass ignorance rather than dub it
a deliberate lie." The second clause, termed "a belated wail,"
concerned the amount voted by City Council for various war
efforts. "This," said Lochead contemptuously, "is no time to pat
our own backs and shout from the house tops how much we are
contributing. Rather it is time to give quietly all we possibly can
and not make a big mouth about it." Besides, what had the
Trades and Labour Council itself contributed? Last fall they'd
actually voted *against* the city granting $20,000 to the Red
Cross. "A truly British spirit of loyalty must have prompted that
resolution!" As for the third clause, about the slowness of
recruiting, yes they were certainly right about that! And what
was the reason? It was because pitiful groups like the Trades
and Labour Council were being obstructionists. If "they had
done a little recruiting in their own ranks, the slowness in joining the colours might not be so glaringly evident in Berlin today.
The T. and L. have about 600 members and about 10 (a little
less than 2%) have donned the khaki. British patriotism must
surely run riot in their ranks that they should make such a
splendid rush to offer themselves to the Empire in her need."
And so it went on, through clause after clause, derision alternat-
ing with indignation, with now and again a quick jab at the
Trades and Labour Council's writing abilities, which are vari-
ously described as "illiterate" and "a literary gem of grammatical
perfection." Behind all these insults, of course, lies the suggestion from the socially superior being that hopelessly uneducated
serfs would do well to remember their place.

Such withering broadsides are intended to send the enemy
skulking off with its tail between its legs, but to Lochead's cha-
grin the Trades and Labour Council was not so easily moved.

The following day they came back with a reply that took the debate to a new level of venom. This reply is interesting chiefly for two reasons. The first is that it is filled with a personal animus against Lochead that is expressed in stronger terms than would probably be acceptable in today's bland press. The libel laws have done wonders for human courtesy. Lochead is referred to as "The Insurance Agent Soldier," and his lack of military expertise is highlighted. "Give us leaders! Men of ability. Soldiers who know what soldiering is. We deem it unwise to hand our bodies over to the keeping of a four-month recruit. If you want to accomplish results in recruiting, get a competent soldier at the head of the regiment." Lochead's defence of his troops' street-recruiting tactics is also vehemently rejected, once again with *ad hominem* slurs: "Since when has compulsion in Berlin or anywhere else in Canada become necessary? From whom has Col. Lochead received the authority to use compulsion on men to join the ranks? The war had been in progress for one year before Col. Lochead was compelled to display his patriotism and he had to get a commission before he would start to scrub the moss off his back and don the khaki. Is this another ignorant misstatement?"

The other interesting feature is that the Trades and Labour Council's reply makes it absolutely clear that it is, indeed, a matter of class antagonisms, of organized labour rejecting a capitalists' war. No surprise is expressed at Lochead's "bitter attack." After all, "he never did have any use or respect for an organization of working men." Reference is made to the years before the war when "our factories were closed and idle. The workers hungry. But oh! so full of patriotism," and the Council's opposition to the City's grant of $20,000 to the Red Cross is justified on the grounds that it was its duty to protect "the interests of the workers, and prevent any increase in taxation. If all the members of the T. and L.," it went on, unable to resist the personal crack, "were fortunate enough to receive a pay envelope every two weeks with the same amount enclosed as that which Col. Lochead receives for the same time, there might not have been any serious objection to the amount of the City's grant." As for patriotism, that most precious word in the lexicon of capitalist war propaganda, "The awful waste that patriotism necessitates ought to be sufficient to cure the man of even average intelligence from this disease and members of the T. and L. Council are not wasters by any means." Patriotism a disease! A waste!

One can almost hear the buttons popping off dress uniforms in officers' messes.

The matter of "race" was raised only once. Lochead had suggested that the author of their resolution was not of British pedigree and, indeed, that the president of the Council was probably an alien and should be interned. Both charges were forcefully rejected. In the case of the former,

> it may please him [Lochead] to know that the ignorant, un-British subject who drew up the T. and L. resolution served several years in the British army, and that in all his military experiences never once heard a soldier cast such insulting remarks towards any organization as Col. Lochead has done to the T. and L. Nor has he seen in any of the British Dominions or British Isles such roughneck tactics indulged in, not even by the toughest element in the regiment, as were displayed on our streets here last Saturday evening. Actions speak louder than words colonel. Go and fight. And then come back and tell us ignorant stay-at-homes how you licked the ignorant Huns!

Lochead, who probably had not expected to unleash such a torrent of abuse, must by now have been feeling slightly clubbed. It was time to retire to the moral high ground, so, wrapping himself in a somewhat biblical mantle, he replied,

> Verily, theirs is a peculiar species of love. Real love is marked by courage, unselfishness and sacrifice and hence these men possess no REAL love — of home, country or apparently of anything else that really counts in life. Let us hope that pure shame, if nothing else, will smite their hearts and induce them to at least keep silent hereafter while others take their place in line.

But it is not surprising that Lochead, rather loftily, wanted to break off this particular engagement with the pesky workers of Berlin. He was becoming embroiled in yet another problem, and though he may not have been the most astute of officers, at least he knew that it was unwise to fight on two fronts at once. Besides, the second cause threatened to become the more important one, if for no other reason than that it put Lochead himself, Berlin, and its racial/recruiting problems onto the wider provincial stage.

Some of the details of the Mayer case are obscure, though its general outlines are clear enough. Lochead had apparently decided that the way to put an end to "pro-Kaiserism" in Berlin once and for all was to go for a test case, in effect to bring a charge of sedition against some fifth-column agitator and to give it as much publicity as possible — pour décourager les autres, so to speak. Unfortunately, up to now he hadn't been able to put together the necessary evidence. As he complained to the *London Advertiser*, "every time I ask for positive proof, for affidavits, the informants closed up tighter than clams, and I could get no proof." Then, around the middle of January, a young man named Alfred Stewart, an employee of the Kaufman Rubber Co., came down to the recruiting office and enlisted. He returned to Kaufman's for a few days while waiting for his papers to be processed, and during this time was accosted by a fellow employee, one Walter Mayer, said to be of German extraction, who, according to Stewart, "outrageously abused him" for joining up and used "the most seditious and disloyal language."

Here was the "positive proof" that Lochead had been waiting for in order to demonstrate that the full weight of the law would be brought to bear on anyone who obstructed recruiting in any way, and he was prepared to stake his reputation on the outcome. He immediately laid a charge against Mayer, who was thrown in jail. When he came up before the local magistrate, Weir, Mayer was remanded for trial at the Spring Assizes and released on $6,000 bail. Then something happened in high places. The crown attorney, W.H. Bowlby, received instructions not to proceed with the case. When he was questioned about this, Bowlby stonewalled. "I received a letter from the attorney-general at Toronto saying that I had been instructed that the Government had dropped the charge. I proceeded on those instructions, and the man did not appear after being remanded. I know little of the case as I was not in police court when he was remanded." Lochead was furious. Sensing "the trail of the serpent of politics," he lashed out in all directions. He was convinced that the malignant influence of pro-Germanism lay behind all his troubles and now, just when he was about to deliver that influence a symbolic, not to say crushing, blow, the authorities for unknown but clearly corrupt reasons were trying (to pile on the metaphors) to whip the carpet out from under him and leave him with egg on his face. His Teutonic tormentors, or the "dirty element," as he called them, *had* to be taught their places. Amongst these, he added in his freewheeling diatribe, were certain Lutheran ministers who had come up from the United States to sow local discord. They "should be drowned or put in jail." (One of these was the ill-fated Rev. Tappert, whom we shall be meeting later.) "It will be impossible to recruit men until they are curbed. Scores of them should be interned. They would be in any other city, but the weakness, or worse, of those in authority has resulted in placing the city of Berlin in a false light in the opinion of the rest of the province." Lochead was very angry indeed. Clearly the time had come for a showdown, and he was prepared to put his military career on the line. "I gave up a good thing financially and socially to take up the duties of commanding officer," he complained to his Board of Trade cronies. "Either Mayer is going to face the music, or I am going to quit."

Thus were colours bravely nailed to the mast. The next move was to go as high as possible in order to seek vindication. To Ottawa. To Sir Sam Hughes himself, the man who had appointed him and who would surely back him up; the only man who could give him back his prestige and his pride, and who also had the necessary weight to counter subversion in high places—if such there were. On Sunday evening, January 30, Lochead was on the 5:55 bound for Ottawa.

It should be said, however, that it is possible that Hughes arranged the meeting, not Lochead. Certainly, the reprehensible recruiting episode of a week earlier in the streets of Berlin had been a national news story, and Sir Sam, who obviously would not want conscription to develop a tarnished image, may have summoned Lochead for an accountability session. There was also the suggestion that Weichel, the Conservative M.P. suspected of playing some sort of byzantine role in the Mayer affair, may have had a word with his war minister colleague in the corridors of power. If this is so, then it is possible that Lochead was using the Mayer case to bolster his contention that he was trying to recruit in what was practically enemy territory, and therefore he and his soldiers were justified in using extreme measures.

Whatever the facts of the situation, Sir Sam, who had rather more pressing matters to attend to, had been briefed on both affairs. His initial response, as Lochead's train sped towards the capital, was standard brass-hat blarney. "Colonel Lochead? Splendid officer! Most enthusiastic! He's done and is doing great work!" Unfortunately his next comment didn't quite contain the fire and brimstone support that his aggrieved junior officer would have preferred to hear. "I must say, though, that the information that has reached us about the Berlin situation isn't quite as serious as Lt. Col. Lochead seems to think. Still he may be right. I'm having a conference with him tomorrow and then we'll see."

It is, of course, impossible to say exactly what transpired at the Monday morning conference. Afterwards, Hughes issued the classic My-Subordinate-Right-Or-Wrong statement, and as for the recruiting problems in general and the infamous Saturday night fracas in particular, all was miraculously made to disappear in a puff of sophistry:

> Col. Lochead saw me today. He tells me that the great majority of German Canadians are intensely loyal, save for an odd man here and there. . . . There is no truth whatsoever in the statement that men are being taken off the streets of Berlin and forced to enlist. In one instance an individual had spoken disrespectfully of a regiment and its officers. Some men who heard him took him to headquarters and forced an apology. That is all there is to it.

This tacit approval of, or at least turning a blind eye on, the 118th's belligerent recruiting methods was to have unhappy repercussions for Berlin.

The Mayer affair, on the other hand, had a resolution that is somewhat mystifying. On Monday, February 1, when Lochead returned from Ottawa he stated enigmatically, "the Mayer case will be satisfactorily adjusted in due time, and in fairness to Mr. W.G. Weichel, M.P., I want it known to those who have hinted that he was connected with the suppression of the case that he had nothing whatsoever to do with it. That is all I have for publication at present." On February 2, the following bulletin was issued from the office of the attorney-general: "Representations from the Militia Department were received here to the effect that as Mayer had already been in jail ten days, his punishment had been sufficient, and that no good purpose could be gained by pressing the prosecution further. The county crown attorney was instructed accordingly." It isn't clear when Mayer was in jail for 10 days, but the day before he came up for the trial that the attorney-general seems to have precluded, he issued a public *mea culpa*:

> Since my arrest I have thought a great deal over my words that were the cause of same and I must say I cannot understand how I came to make the statement I did. . . . Whatever punishment I may have to suffer for my foolish language I will nevertheless from now on openly encourage recruiting and will do whatever I can on every occasion to prove that I am a faithful subject of our King. When I come up for trial I shall plead guilty and I will recognize that any punishment that I have undergone, or may

be called upon to undergo, will be for the general good of Canadians.

And so on for several more abject sentences. One can only guess
at what pressures lay behind this remarkable example of crow-
eating. It could almost have been composed by Lochead himself
for Mayer's signature; perhaps when a man has been in jail for a
fortnight it tends to concentrate the mind wonderfully. At his
trial Mayer was found guilty and immediately released on promise of good behaviour.

One senses here much in the way of pleas being bargained,
deals struck, troubled waters oiled, and at least for Lochead,
faces saved and honours satisfied. But in the midst of the Mayer
brouhaha Berlin got some no doubt welcome relief from its
ordeals when national attention was turned for a few days to a
much more sensational event. On February 3, the Parliament
buildings in Ottawa were destroyed by fire.

The fire started at 8:50 p.m. in the Reading Room. At the
time, W.S. Loggie, the member for Northumberland, N.B., was
making a speech about the Atlantic fisheries which, fortunately,
was not at that time the most rivetting of topics, and as a result
there were only about 20 members in the chamber. Then the
door burst open and someone (many claimed the credit) rushed
in and shouted that a fire had broken out. Some members,
though startled, didn't initially react with the speed that the situation in fact warranted. Several began to clear out their desks,
and one, assuming it was a minor and remote inconvenience,
started to read a newspaper. Within a minute the corridor outside was filled with smoke. Of the many confusing stories that
were told of that night, one fact was agreed upon by all. The fire
spread with incredible rapidity through the old building, with its
wooden floors and panelling. Weichel, who was enjoying a quiet
cigar in the third-floor restaurant, described the scene in words
that, though perhaps touched up for dramatic effect, were probably not far off the mark. "Pillars of flame rushed like racing
horses down the corridors and round corners. Tongues of flame
seemed simultaneously to leap out of everywhere."

There were many tales of small heroisms, close escapes, and
tragedies. Burrell, the minister of agriculture, whose office
adjoined the Reading Room, had to make his escape through the
worst of the fire and was badly burned. Those caught in the
upper restaurant found the stairways blocked by smoke. They
ran to the south-west corner of the building where, 60 feet up,
they called for help from the crowds milling around in the dark-

The Battle for Berlin

ness below. In the race between the ladders and the flames, the ladders won by about 15 minutes. Two Saskatchewan M.P.s, McNutt and Cash, "were in the lavatory when the fire assumed big proportions." They appear to have effected their escape through a handy window by tying towels together and thereby just reaching a ladder thrust up from outside. Madame Sevigny, the Speaker's wife, was in her apartment entertaining two Quebec ladies. She managed to pack her two children and their nurses off, and then turned her attention to her guests, Madames Bray and Morin. She led them to a window where they could jump into a fire net, but the two ladies elected to return for their fur coats. Both died. Sir Robert Borden made a hasty exit from his office minus hat and coat. And hatless and coatless were most of the members as they stumbled out into the icy cold of the night, their jackets over their heads, handkerchiefs over their mouths, coughing and wheezing as they fought to expel the acrid smoke. Seven people lost their lives.

The question on everyone's lips almost immediately was, How did the fire start? Although there does not ever seem to have been a definitive answer, it is difficult not to speculate that the cause was a cigar butt or a wayward match thoughtlessly discarded in the Reading Room, and that the stacks of paper, the oiled-pine woodwork, the varnished oak, and the drafty corridors did the rest. But such mundane explanations are never satisfying to a nation in the grip of war fever. Clearly it was a dastardly enemy plot. The definite assertion that "the conflagration was the work of incendiaries and it is confidently believed that they are Germans," whipped through the country as fast as the flames through the building. Sir Wilfrid Laurier, leader of the Opposition, categorically blamed "the disciples of German kultur" for the tragedy.

Fuelled by the media's desire for sinister stories, people began to see spies and terrorists with even greater frequency than before, and for the next few days tales of sabotage proliferated. Disguised German officers were said to be lurking on the border, ready to invade Canada and seize the Welland canal. (There was obviously something of an obsession about the strategic importance of this particular waterway.) There were said to be caches of Mauser rifles dotted about the countryside. In Wingham, Adolphe Schatte, having been observed unloading camouflaged goods from his car, was arrested on suspicion of being an enemy agent. He turned out to be the conductor of the Wingham band, transporting musical instruments. There was a fire at a Hespeler munitions plant, and John Schmidt, an Austrian, was taken into custody. A shadowy figure was seen crossing the ice towards the Victoria Bridge in Montreal, obviously with the intent of blowing it up. None of these stories ever seemed to lead anywhere, but they serve as a reminder that the bogeyman in the black cape and mask, clutching a round bomb with a fizzing fuse, is as much a constant of war as political rhetoric and civilian death.

One more story. A man with a funny foreign accent was noted leaving Ottawa hurriedly by train shortly after the fire. The telegraph wires hummed furiously and the train was stopped just as it was about to cross the border between Windsor and Detroit. The man was apprehended in the saloon car, and when picture postcards of the Parliament buildings were found in his possession, the case for inviting him to spend the night in jail was complete. The next day he was discovered to be a Belgian pianist and conductor, Charles Strony, in the event an extremely angry Charles Strony, who had been in Ottawa accompanying Mme. Louise Edvina in a concert before the Governor-General at the time of the fire, and who had been on his way to Chicago to conduct the Chicago Grand Opera Company, a date that his arrest had forced him to miss. Despite being released immediately, the gallant though fuming little Belgian promised to return at some future date in order to sue the Canadian government.

The net result of the Ottawa conflagration was to further increase Canadian distaste for all things German. This was not some remote atrocity, but an attack on the nation's seat of government, right here at home. As the man in the Ottawa street contemptuously asserted, "they know in Berlin by now that their reprisals on Canada have started." Berlin! The very name, chosen with such pride 83 years earlier by a small Ontario town, was becoming a serious liability due to guilt by association. On February 4, the day after the fire, an awkward and anonymous letter appeared in the *News-Record*:

> As a citizen and ratepayer I want a resolution put before the Council to some member or members to change the name of the town and want the members' votes recorded when the resolution is put. There is no need of the Council wasting time arguing this matter. Put the resolution.
>
> A Ratepayer

FOUR

Change the Name!

Not that the letter to the *News-Record* made a particularly novel suggestion. As early as November 1914 the *Windsor Record* had rather cheekily proposed the same thing, and sniping of a similar nature had continued intermittently ever since. The *Telegraph* had floated the idea after the sinking of the *Lusitania* in 1915; a Toronto newspaper had chipped in with the thought that "one would hardly expect a town with such a name as Berlin to have an efficient sewage system"; and two days before the Ottawa fire the *St. Thomas Times* had wondered "why we should perpetuate in Ontario the name of the capital city of the arch-fiend." Indeed, Berliners had every reason to believe that censorious Ontario eyes were upon them, and one can hazard the guess that wherever two or three of the city's movers and shakers (mainly Board of Trade members), were gathered together—over the postprandial brandy perhaps or having whiskers snipped in the DeBus tonsorial parlour or maybe standing at the urinals of city hall—there was many a furious muttering about the indignity of living in a city with such an odious name. Up to now these pressures from within and without had been sporadic, but the Ottawa fire changed all that. It was the catalyst that finally set in motion the campaign to change Berlin's name.

But before going any further it will be helpful to say a bit more about the three public bodies that had most influence on the lives of Berliners—the Board of Trade, the Trades and Labour Council, and the City Council—their composition, and how they related to each other. The Board of Trade, founded in 1886, was of course composed of the most influential men in town, or those who aspired to be. Their sole concern was Berlin's economic well-being, and as they believed that this was the only well-being worth bothering with, they assumed a divine right to dictate policy to all and sundry. In 1914 they had tried, with supreme arrogance, to get the City Council abolished in favour of a commission (basically consisting of their own members) that would run Berlin in a way that was, as Patricia McKegney nicely puts it, "congenial to their manner of thinking." The most zealous leaders in the twin campaigns to change the name and raise a battalion were members of this body, and it was their brashness and general contempt for the democratic process that was to characterize the way the campaigns were conducted.

The Trades and Labour Council had been formed in 1900. As has been recounted, it did not by any means see eye to eye with the Board of Trade on recruiting, let alone conscription, and it was, not surprisingly, not nearly as keen about voting money for the various war funds as the wealthier organization. Apart from this, they were not a militant group unless provoked and, generally speaking, shared in the communal desire to promote the interests of Busy Berlin.

It was in the third body, the City Council, that the first two came together. The City Council consisted of a mayor and 15 aldermen. The mayor, recently acclaimed for a second term, was Dr. J.E. Hett. His specialty, one in which he became rather too wrapped up in later years, was cancer. Round-cheeked and, though still in his thirties, already quite bald, he had something of the appearance of a billiard ball with a moustache. He was a popular man who had originally been elected by a working-class vote, and at the end of his first term when he treated his alderman to a meal at Gettas and Gettas he had been serenaded with "For He's A Jolly Good Fellow." Within a few months the cry would be "Off with his head!" but such are the vagaries of politics. Of the 15 aldermen, about half were Board of Trade men. Of these, we have already met Cleghorn. The two who almost invariably seconded his motions were Irvine Master, of the City Flour Mill Co., and J.A. Hallman, of the Walker Bin & Fixture Co. There was one other physician, H.H. Huehnergard, and one dentist, A.E. Rudell, who were solidly in the Cleghorn camp. The three Trades and Labour Council men were John Reid, its current president; Gallagher (though he was upwardly mobile and had recently also joined the Board of Trade); and C.C. Hahn. Hahn had been mayor five years earlier, at the time the youngest mayor in Ontario, and clearly thought that he should still be mayor. His portrait as mayor shows a man with staring eyes and a priggish tilt to the chin. By 1915, as an alderman, he had changed his hairstyle, but the eyes remained the same, and his soft features now gave him the appearance of a slightly defensive storefront mannequin. Finally there was the inimitable David Gross. He began his working life in a button factory which, when it fell on evil days, he took over with some fellow workers and eventually owned outright. Excitable and independent, he was a favourite with his workers and had come top of the aldermanic poll. The waves of hair that rose from his forehead gave him the appearance of a man battling into a high wind, which in truth he had to do a lot of in the coming months — most of the wind usually emanating from Cleghorn or Hahn. It is doubtful whether any of these aldermen realized when they were elected on January 1, 1916, that they were in for the stormiest year of their lives.

Early in February 1916, then, a small group of men had decided that the time had come to make a concerted effort to get rid of the name Berlin. Their first problem was to figure out a way of doing this as swiftly and with as little public input as possible. Obviously there would be quite a bit of resistance to such a move, either due to misguided sentiment or, more ominously, because there was a lot of "pro-Hun" sentiment floating about, so what was needed was a carefully orchestrated, emotional blitzkrieg that would both pre-empt any sort of serious counter-offensive and also demonstrate to the uncommitted, to City Council, and subsequently to the provincial government, that the vast majority supported the move.

During the week following the Ottawa fire the word was put out that there would be "a citizens' meeting" on the afternoon of Friday, February 11, in the Council Chamber at city hall. The converted were particularly urged to attend, but in order to avoid the charge of railroading, one or two prominent citizens whose attitudes were less certain were also invited. Louis Breithaupt for example. As a former mayor, president of the Breithaupt Leather Co., president of the German School Society, director of the Economical Mutual Fire Insurance Co., first Vice-President of the Berlin Patriotic Fund (and father of a future Lieutenant-Governor) he and his extensive family had a certain standing in the community. Obviously such a man, though suspected of being a wet on the issue of changing Berlin's name, could not be ignored, though perhaps he could be kept slightly in the dark about the exact nature and purpose of the meeting that, as Breithaupt confided in his diary, "was not publicly advertised and therefore not in a real sense a public meeting."

He was under the impression that it was to be an exploratory forum at which a fair cross-section of Berliners would be able to air their views about the pros and cons of a name change in an atmosphere of sweetness and light. What he found instead was a packed meeting (charged with sourness and spite), a pre-selected chairman, and a pre-written petition to City Council:

> WHEREAS it would appear that a strong prejudice has been created throughout the British Empire against the name "Berlin" and all that the name implies,
>
> AND WHEREAS the citizens of the City fully appreciate that this prejudice is but natural, it being absolutely impossible for any loyal citizen to consider it complimentary to be longer called after the Capital of Prussia,
>
> BE IT THEREFORE AND IT IS HEREBY RESOLVED that the City Council be petitioned to take the necessary steps to have the name "BERLIN" changed to some other name more in keeping with our National sentiment.

The ensuing "debate" oscillated between mawkish sentiment, moralistic claptrap, and righteous indignation. Words like "degradation," "stigma," and "atrocities" flew freely about the room. The rape of Belgian womanhood, babies impaled on Prussian bayonets, the slaughter of the innocent passengers of the *Lusitania* were all said somehow to blacken the name of Berlin, Ontario. Even Edith Cavell was worked in as a reason for changing the name. The fatuous vied with the non-sequitur in the struggle for the truth. D. Hibner claimed that changing the name would be a tremendous slap in the face for the enemy. George DeBus eagerly pointed out that it would be easy to change the name — after all, Kenora had done so because it used to be called Rat Portage. Then there was the destruction of the Parliament buildings, the cause of which, though officially unknown, was here definitively claimed to be the work of enemy aliens. This was too much for the combative Nick Asmussen who, like Gross, had worked his way up from labourer to owner of his own company and who, much later in this story, was to become the victim of mob violence, and later still, an M.P.P. and mayor of the city. He angrily protested that there was no such proof, that the fire had nothing whatsoever to do with the name of the city, and then went on to commit the terrible heresy of questioning the accuracy of the stories about German atrocities. This put the meeting in an uproar. and he was furiously told to go and read the Bryce report that proved beyond the shadow of a doubt the truth of "Hun" barbarities.

The fact that the aforesaid report was a pack of lies put out by the British propaganda machine was neither here nor there. (Though it is interesting to note Modris Eksteins's contention that it was the Germans "who most blatantly stretched international standards of behaviour and morality" [p. 188] in methods of combat.) Scepticism, let alone truth, are unwelcome guests in wartime. As for the Ottawa fire, Asmussen was magisterially rebuked by Williams, who assured him that he knew for a fact that the conflagration was "Hun" inspired. His "proof" was that he was in Ottawa at the time. This assertion was received with great applause, and when Asmussen tried to reply he was howled down.

When Breithaupt rose to speak he began by expressing his uneasiness about the way the meeting had been set up. "I didn't know very much about this meeting. In fact I was surprised at the notice which I received, for the purpose of it was not stated. I had no idea that the resolution was cut and dried before the meeting." Characteristically his appeal was for moderation. "Let us not become hysterical, or be stampeded into anything which in more sober moments we might regret. This city has been proud of its name for ninety years. Surely we are not going to change it without a great deal of thought. I am British and am proud to be so, but what am I to do with my name? Should I change it? What are you going to do with all the other German names of our neighbouring towns — with Baden, New Hamburg and Breslau; with Hanover and Bamberg? Are you going to change them too?" Breithaupt was supported with considerable passion, not to say bluntness, by Rev. J. Lynn, a Presbyterian minister. "This attempt to change the name of our city under existing conditions is pure childishness and I say not fair. Let me tell you moreover that whatever you may call it wont make a particle of difference as far as recruiting is concerned." He went on to exhort people to remember the honourable history of the community, but needless to say the pleas for moderation were easily swamped by the voices of irrationality. One of these belonged to A.A. Eby, the mover of the resolution, and the great-grandson of the man who had first given the hamlet its name, who announced with sublime, atavistic authority that "if Benjamin Eby were living today he would be delighted to have the name changed."

The petition passed easily, "the only dissenting voices," as Breithaupt sadly commented in his diary, "being Mr. Asmussen, Rev. Mr. Lynn and myself. Mr. Asmussen was the only one who voted against the proposition—some few not voting at all." Interestingly enough, the next day Breithaupt's name appeared on the list of those who had supported the petition, and again he had to protest. "I beg to state that at the meeting at the City Hall on Friday last I signed a paper supposed to be a list of those in attendance. I am now informed that the said paper is in reality the petition itself. My remarks at the meeting, however, explained my position." Whether this was trickery or merely an excess of zeal on the part of the name-changers is hard to say.

On the day following this "public" meeting, the emotional temperature in Berlin was raised a few more degrees when Captain Dancey made a return appearance at the recruiting gabfests held every Saturday in the Roma and Star Theatres—invited of course by the same gentlemen who were behind the name-changing campaign. Dancey, who wrote bad novels and also claimed that he was a secret agent and had operated behind enemy lines and witnessed the atrocities that he was so fond of describing, was a professional demagogue whose specialty was whipping up hatred towards specific groups or, even better, individuals.

Dancey spoke at the afternoon session ("for men only") at the Roma Theatre. The audience was warmed up in the usual way with rousing movies such as *England Expects* and a satire on the German army called *Herr Von Gutz*, presumably a forerunner of television sitcoms like *Hogan's Heroes*, and then the fiery Irishman took the stage. He began with the standard descriptions of the "blood-thirsty, immoral, dastardly outrages which Hun officers and men perpetrated on the women and children of Belgium," and then turned his attentions to Berlin's pathetic recruiting efforts. "Here you have about 20,000 people," he snorted angrily, "and you have not given more than 200 men to the cause! Stratford has given 1,700 men! If you do not give more you will be forever damned in the sight of Canada!" Warming to his theme, he next turned his attention to the snakes in the local bosom. "There are men in this community who cheer German successes when thousands of true British hearts are stilled. They applaud when outrages like the *Lusitania* incident are committed. These men are traitors and cowards and should be placed behind bars." Obviously well briefed about the previous day's meeting (or maybe he had attended it himself), he then proceeded to name names. Asmussen was attacked, as was Breithaupt. "He said the name of Berlin had stood for ninety years and we should not change it in ninety minutes! But how long did it take the Kaiser to change the laws of God and Mankind which have stood for all time?" And finally he vented his wrath on a local Lutheran clergyman, the ill-fated Rev. Tappert.

> You have a minister in your midst by the name of Tappert. This minister's remarks are undoubtedly pro-German! Why do you allow him to run free to make them? The time is coming when he will no longer be a guest of Canada, and it cannot come too soon. Let him get back among the Germans of the United States where he belongs! (Cheers)

Presumably the cheers would have come most strongly from the lads of the 118th, whose attendance at these recruiting meetings was compulsory. Already frustrated by their inability to recruit the smug youth of the city, and smarting from the negative reaction to their loyal efforts, they were now poised like greyhounds in the slips. To these men Dancey's heated words were a clear exhortation to get out there and do something. Anything. And what about Colonel Lochead, who had sat behind Dancey at the meeting, smiling and nodding his head, particularly when Tappert was excoriated? Didn't this amount to tacit approval for a spot of creative vigilantism? For the next three days there was much heated chatter in the barracks. Something should be done about Tappert. He should be run out of town. Tarred and feathered. What about some other targets? The Concordia Singing Society, for example. Now there was a nest of Prussian lovers, if ever there was one. Hadn't they salvaged the bust of old Kaiser Bill after it had been dumped into the lake in Victoria Park? There it was sitting in their club rooms above the Grand Theatre all safe and sound. Who knew what unpatriotic rituals were performed in front of this Hun icon. To seize a trophy like that would be a splendid gesture, and probably a bit safer than assaulting an actual human being.

At about eight o'clock on Tuesday evening, February 15 (at the same time, ironically, that Breithaupt was attending a nearby lecture, entitled "Our Next Door Neighbour" about Berlin's love of law and order) a mob of some 40 or 50 soldiers, well fortified with alcohol, "escaped the vigilance of their officers," and set off for the Concordia Society's rooms to capture the hated statue. Finding the doors locked, they administered a few well-aimed kicks, burst in, located the bust where it had been stored away, and hauled it out into the street. Down King Street they marched, stopping every now and again to sing

"Rule Britannia" and "God Save The King," joyously beating out the time with sticks and canes on the bronze helmet. When they got to the post office, opposite city hall, they turned round and paraded back to the skating rink on Queen Street South, where they knew they would find lots of young men of military age, and their young ladies, waltzing around the ice. Here they held a flashlight to the impassive metal face and delivered recruiting speeches interspersed with more songs. Unfortunately, the band drowned out their best efforts, and the skaters ignored them, so they returned drunkenly to their barracks and locked up their prize in the detention room.

But the night was still young, and the little escapade had been great fun. Maybe there were more German artefacts that could be given similar treatment. So back they went to the Concordia Club again (still escaping the vigilance of their officers — though Lochead had had a brief word with them at the barracks), and this time found a number of pictures of German royalty plus several German flags. These were taken up to the recruiting office on King Street, where the pictures were smashed to smithereens and the flags torn to ribbons and stamped into the snow, "several young ladies," according to the *News-Record*, "aiding heartily in the latter operation. Pieces of the flags were passed around among the bystanders as souvenirs. These were eagerly sought and soon, to fill the demand, the pieces were so small they could have been hidden in a thimble."

By now the soldiers had worked themselves up into a frenzy of destruction, so it was back for a third time to the ill-fated club (still, amazingly, escaping their vigilant officers) where some more flags were ferreted out, plus some German hymn books together with some red, white, and black bunting — and a picture of King George V draped with a German flag. This latter find proved to be what the *News-Record* called

> the red rag to the bull. The soldiers just simply took the brakes off and cut loose. All the pictures of German personages were torn from the walls, smashed to pieces, and strewn around the rooms. The furniture was attacked, tables, chairs, metal ornaments, stage fixtures, bar fixtures, bunting, and, in fact, everything that could be smashed or ripped to pieces was attended to. All windows and glass doors were smashed out, while broken chairs, bunting, hymn books and ornaments were hurled

into the street below. The piano was battered to pieces and lay amidst a wreck of broken furniture, hymn books, playing cards and debris.

In the street below, soldiers and civilians began to make a pile of the flotsam as it came sailing through the windows, and when they had a tidy heap they poured gasoline over it and set it alight. Two drums came bouncing down the stairs and out onto the street, but they were retrieved by "Pop" Phillips to whom they belonged. Much more promising were the three beer kegs that followed the drums. Two, alas, turned out to be empty, but the third was partly full, and it was quickly grabbed by a soldier who tried to run off with it. He was quickly overtaken by his mates and relieved of his load, but unfortunately everyone was too eager to get at the contents. The keg was smashed open on the street and the beer flowed out into the trampled snow.

The bonfire, meanwhile, was blazing merrily away and was being fed by additional bits and pieces still falling in showers from the rooms above. Souvenir hunters, a euphemism for looters, made off with whatever they could lay their hands on – plates, silver ornaments, ashtrays, piano keys. One small boy was observed trying, unsuccessfully, to button his coat around a huge glass dish which he'd managed to partially wrap up in some towels. On King Street the street cars and other traffic were backed up for blocks due to the fire and the crowds, and in nearby alleys five cautious policemen were quietly proving that discretion is the better part of valour – though the official line was that "the affair was over so quickly that they did not have time to interfere." Eventually some vigilant officers of the 118th made their appearance and the troops were quickly rounded up and marched back to the barracks.

The reactions of the authorities, both in Ottawa and Berlin, to the evening's rampage ran the usual gamut from huff to puff. In the House, Sam Hughes read the Riot Act and sternly pointed the finger of blame – though not at those whom one might have supposed to be the culprits. The whole mess was clearly the fault of people like Asmussen and Tappert, who had goaded the soldier boys past endurance. On the home front there was a Court of Inquiry conducted by four of the battalion's officers. Various sergeants, corporals, and privates were cross-examined, but all suffered from the amnesia that traditionally strikes in such situations. Fairly typical was Private Quinn, who was probably in B Company:

Q: Tell us in a few words as to your whereabouts last night.
A: I don't know any of the fellows here at all.
Q: You helped carry the bust down, didn't you?
A: No sir.
Q: Did you see the bust?
A: I saw the bust coming down the street and I followed the procession.
Q: What men out of D Company were carrying it?
A: I don't think any were, sir.
Q: Who were the B Company men?
A: I don't know any of their names.
Q: You ought to know the names of B Company!
A: We all go by "Buddy."
Q: Were you drunk last night?
A: I had a few drinks, sir.
Q: What other men helped break up the chairs and tables?
A: I don't know. I knew them as "Buddy."
Q: Did you see any A Company men there?
A: I can't say. I know them as "Buddy."
Q: Did you see any Machine Gun Section men there?
A: There was a few of them fellows there.
Q: How did you know they were Machine Gun?
A: I saw one fellow there. I think he was Machine Gun.

In the face of such doggedness, it is not surprising to find that the inquiry's fifth conclusion was "That this Court cannot fix individual responsibility for destruction of property." Thus it was that Lochead, in summarizing the episode, was able to tell his fellow citizens that though of course soldiers in uniform were subject to all the penalties of the law, it would unfortunately be impossible to prosecute individuals, not only because no one knew who they were, but also because many ordinary citizens were also involved in the night's lawlessness, and it would, therefore, be difficult to separate the goats from the goats, and anyway it was all the fault of Dancey's rabble-rousing, not to mention local hotel keepers who had sold his men liquor, but on the other hand he wasn't going to declare their establishments out-of-bounds because that wouldn't be fair to the 98 soldiers who had not participated in the shenanigans . . . and so on and so forth.

Not that Lochead was being entirely disingenuous when he referred to civilian participation. One of the fascinating aspects of those troubled times in Berlin is the shadowy role that a group of women, primarily army wives, are supposed to have played. By all accounts their leader was a certain Lil Garner, whose husband Sam, a sergeant, had already gone overseas. Lil, a big, beefy woman, remains a vivid memory for one eyewitness. He was standing near her on the platform of the Victoria St. station, and for some reason her words, to a friend or relation she was seeing off to the war, stuck in his youthful mind. "Stand your ground, Charlie," she said, "stand your ground! Don't run when the Germans come!" This formidable lady was also a keen dispenser of yellow chalk to school children, who were then urged to put stripes down the backs of overcoats of unwary pedestrians. Another suggestion assigns the leadership role to Agnes, Blood's wife, but whatever the truth of the matter, the existence of a platoon of Lady Macbeths egging on their more cautious husbands to commit deeds of mayhem now has something of the status of myth. It is said that in the Concordia riot one woman was so carried away by patriotic zeal that she hitched up her skirts and urinated on the German flag.

Occasionally there was merriment in the midst of the bitterness, such as when Stephen Leacock gave a lecture on Saturday, February 19, four days after the sack of the Concordia Club, that kept the audience "in roars of laughter until one feared that some of them would do themselves an injury," but such comic relief was short-lived. The recruiting battles, Dancey's speech, and the Concordia incident all signalled a deteriorating situation, and it was in this climate of tension and turmoil that the City Council met on Monday evening, February 21, to consider the petition from the earlier "public" meeting. Rumours abounded that not only was Council approval certain, but even that a new name for the city had already been chosen. This fear was not unfounded, as several members of the Board of Trade who had instigated the earlier meeting were also aldermen— Cleghorn, Zettel, Hallman, Rudell, Master, Gallagher—and their intention of pushing the whole thing through with as little public debate as possible had already been established. In the circumstances it is surprising that the *News-Record* was of the opinion a week before that "it is doubtful whether the Mayor and City Council will adopt the proposal, the advantages of which are not clear." No doubt the *News-Record* had taken soundings when it made this optimistic prognosis, but in the following days one may imagine that many an aldermanic arm was twisted, and many an ear bent—and no doubt the fate of the Concordia Club had persuaded the waverers that any hint of pro-Germanism was, quite simply, dangerous.

There were no absentees when Mayor Hett called the meeting to order at eight o'clock. The name-changers had also made sure that the public seating was packed with vociferous supporters. There was confusion almost immediately, when Mayor Hett (himself almost certainly opposed to the change, though desperate to appear neutral and keep the peace) blandly announced that there were not one but two motions before the meeting. The first, moved and seconded by Cleghorn and Hallman, was to change the name. The second, sponsored by Schnarr and Reid, called for consideration of the merits of amalgamation with Waterloo. Hett read the Schnarr motion first and invited him to speak to it, which he began to do, but Cleghorn was immediately on his feet exclaiming angrily, "What about my motion?" Presumably he smelt, no doubt correctly, a delaying tactic, for the old chestnut of amalgamation would take weeks if not months of negotiations and committees, and the hyped-up campaign for change could well fizzle out like a damp squib.

For the next half-hour the aldermen wrangled about whose motion got onto the order paper first, whether one could be an amendment to the other, which one should take logical precedence, and so on. To add to the confusion, but rather cunningly, Aldermen Hahn and Gallagher moved that the audience be allowed to chip in with their two cents worth. This was the occasion for a number of emotional digressions from the floor, a lot of political flim flam, some personal insults and boasts about who had or had not got sons in the army, and a challenge from Gross directed at some particularly obstreperous member of the audience. (During the year Gross would issue more challenges than a quarrelsome Restoration gallant.) The upshot of this noisy barrage was that Schnarr rather sheepishly agreed to allow the Cleghorn motion to be discussed first.

There is no need to rehearse the arguments that were trotted out in this part of the debate. They followed the well-worn assertions about the dishonour attached to the name of Berlin, and the counter-claims that the dishonour lay not in the name, but in the inability of the city to raise a battalion, and that changing the name would have no effect whatsoever on this crucial recruiting issue. Finally a standing vote was taken on the resolution. "Moved, that a Petition be forthwith presented to the Local Legislature praying that an Act be passed at the approaching session of the Legislative Assembly changing the name of the Corporation of the City of Berlin." The result was predictable — though the *News-Record* claimed "that it caused some surprise, several aldermen having changed their previous opinions." Thirteen men rose in favour, and two remained obstinately seated in spite of considerable abuse and the veiled threat that "if you oppose the change it will always be an incumbrance on you. It will break your neck." Those who voted for the resolution (note the ethnic origins of the names) were Huehnergard, Zettel, Schwartz, Hahn, Hessenauer, Dunke, Rudell, Schnarr, Master, Gallagher, Ferguson, Hallman, and Cleghorn. The two opposed were Gross and Reid.

Finally, the petition to investigate the feasibility of amalgamation with Waterloo came before the meeting. There was little discussion. Everyone was too tired. It passed unanimously.

The next 10 days was a period of frantic manoeuvrings, which saw those in favour of the name change trying to maintain the momentum of their initial success in the face of the first real signs of serious opposition to their campaign. On Friday, February 25, there was another meeting of the City Council, at which the main item of business was the method by which a new name should be chosen. The egregious Cleghorn was of the opinion that, with 1,080 signatures on a petition to change the name, it surely wasn't necessary to consult the public further. He demanded that a special committee be appointed forthwith consisting of five members from Council, three from the Public School Board, one from the Collegiate Board, one from the Separate School Board, and five from the Board of Trade. This committee would select four or five names, one of which they would recommend to the City Council for ratification. A neat, simple, oligarchic solution that would in effect put the decision in Board of Trade hands. Mayor Hett, however, bravely dug in his heels on the issue. Though a committee to select the slate of names seemed to him reasonable, he insisted that the matter should finally be put to a public vote. But a public vote was something the name-changers did not desire; such a democratic procedure was much too chancy. The matter of amalgamation with Waterloo also again came up for discussion, and on this occasion took precedence. It was finally decided to hold another meeting to formulate plans on amalgamation, and Cleghorn's despotic proposal was put on hold.

Meanwhile, objections not only to the methods being proposed for changing the name, but also to changing the name at all were beginning to appear in the daily press. One letter argued that 1,080 names didn't represent all the ratepayers and applauded Mayor Hett's insistence on a plebiscite. A second suggested that many had been forced to sign the petition against their will. A third, from William Kingsley, a militant socialist worker, promised that "We working men will give you a race to see who is running this city. I ask in the name of a working man not to place our names on such a ridiculous petition and run still further into the hole by spending thousands of dollars wholly uncalled for." A fourth stated that a counter-petition was beginning to circulate, and that it also contained 1,000 names. But the most reasoned argument against changing the name came from W.H. Breithaupt, an engineer, president of the Waterloo County Historical Society, and the brother of L.J. Breithaupt. Appropriately enough he began his letter with a short history on the relativity of historical associations. Berlin, he pointed out, was not originally named after the capital of the German Empire, because there was no such thing at the time. It was simply a major city of a country that, indeed, happened to be an ally of Britain during the Napoleonic Wars. He suggested that there were many other names of German origin that had become Canadian or British — Guelph, for example, or "the name of our illustrious Royal family." To start changing names because of ephemeral historical events was obviously ridiculous: "Will it make any difference whatever in the cause now most important and most compelling of all, that of British success in the war? Will it not rather demonstrate our lack of dignity and make us a butt of derision from one end of the country to the other?" He then went on to argue passionately that there is no contradiction in being both proud of one's heritage and loyal to one's country.

> We are of German descent, and are not ashamed of it . . . but . . . though of German descent we are not Germans, nor are we German-Canadians or any other variety of Germans or part Germans; not hyphenates as Mr Weichel has well said. We are Canadians, and yield not an iota to anyone in devotion to our country and to the ideals of the British Empire.

He then very neatly turned the tables on the opposition and its authoritarian tactics.

> The change of the name of our good City is something that affects many of us lightly. To others of us, perhaps more of us, it is a question of vital concern. Under British institutions, on which we pride ourselves, there is a well established method of ascertaining the will of the governed, and that is by ballot. . . . Or shall we admit that Prussian ideals of government have

already so far impressed us that we are ready to adopt them, ready to impose the will of the few on the many; of the minority on the majority.

He concluded by casting doubt on the legitimacy of the much vaunted petition of 1,080 names collected by the name-changers.

> Let there be eliminated all the names not on the City's voters' lists, as such names clearly are on the petition without right. If further there be scratched all names of those to whom the question is wholly indifferent and who signed in complaisance merely; and also all those who signed through coercion, such as by a factory proprietor personally making a round of his employees; and lastly such who for any reason would now vote differently. . . . [T]hen let us see what would remain of this sole mandate under which the change of name is to go forward.

Potentially this was an extremely damaging letter, not simply because it came from such a respected source, but also because its nice combination of reason and passion could help to focus the opposition to the name change. Obviously there had to be some quick damage control. Two replies followed almost immediately. The first was an emotional piece from A.A. Eby recounting the story of a distant business man who refused to buy Berlin goods because he had two sons at the front. The second, predictably, was from Cleghorn, a man who seems to have had well-developed attack instincts, though his letter is so outrageous in its fieriness that it is comic. He begins by saying that he's fed up with hearing about all the achievements of the early German settlers. "They came from Germany to a veritable garden at an opportune time and prospered." The image of early settlers rolling into a land already cultivated and flowing with milk and honey is delightful, but perhaps it's a predictable sentiment from this prickly Scot. "But this is not the time," he goes on, "to deal in quibbles as to whether Berlin was built by Germans, by English, Irish, Canadians or the Breithaupts." What we are fighting here is "the German Empire whence have emanated the most diabolical crimes and atrocities that have marred the pages of history; an empire that has allied with the murderous, barbarous, unspeakable Turk to help to force its ideas of 'Kultur' on the whole world." But enough of generalities. It is the credibility of Breithaupt himself that needs to be savaged. "How many of his name . . . are today fighting in the cause of liberty?" Worse still, up to the present time, Mr. Breithaupt and those whom he assumes to represent, have not only taken no part in recruiting, but have apparently discouraged it in certain quarters; otherwise why should not their families be represented on the honour roll of their country? Is it fair to say "Let us do our duty to King and Country" while your own kith and kin stand around and let other boys go forth to fight their battles?

He ends with a dazzling accusation and a veiled threat.

In conclusion we would say that even if the question of the change of name of Berlin were submitted to a vote of the people it would afford very little satisfaction to Mr. Breithaupt, as he would have no say in the matter. The Recruiting Committee has evidence that Mr. Breithaupt is not a British subject, and is therefore an alien, and would not be entitled to a vote on this question. Such being the case it should have behooved Mr. Breithaupt to keep silent. Has he been voting illegally all these years? Is he today qualified for the municipal office which he holds?

Though constitutionally unsuited to political mudslinging, and no doubt slightly surprised by the vituperation that he had unleashed, this was a little too much for W.H. Breithaupt. His family had been in Berlin for two generations, and though it is true that he had been born in the States (which was the source of Cleghorn's mud) and spent the first few years of his working life there, he had lived in Berlin for 30 years, and was certainly eligible to vote and hold public office. He instructed his lawyer, H.J. Sims, to request a retraction or else to sue. As no more is heard of the matter, one can assume that Cleghorn backed down. As for the lack of recruits from the Breithaupt family, there were five of military age at this time, one of whom, William Walter, L.J. Breithaupt's son, enlisted a year later. The nastiness of the affair must have upset the Breithaupt brothers, particularly as it had involved their families, and L.J. Breithaupt in effect bowed out of the game. Indeed, his name and that of his company appear on later pro-change propaganda, and one therefore has to conclude that, for one reason or another, he swerved from his earlier convictions. This left W.H. Breithaupt as one of the few men of stature in Berlin prepared to continue the fight, a fight which, it was becoming increasingly clear, would require not only moral, but also physical courage. But whether fortunately or unfortunately, Breithaupt was a courteous and reasonable man and his low-key approach was often not heard. In the battle for attention it is always the strident bombast of the huckster that, initially at any rate, seduces the uncommitted.

Not that Breithaupt was without his supporters, one of whom, the rough and ready Kingsley, was quite prepared to meet Cleghorn on his own terms. He derided Cleghorn's hypocrisy and asked how many of the sons of "your party" had escaped to the States to avoid enlistment. He also somewhat saucily invited Cleghorn to enlist himself—which was pushing it a bit, as Cleghorn was 54 at the time. As for changing the name of the city, he ended his letter with the clinching argument: "If you change the name of Limburger cheese would it change the smell?" Perhaps he might have found a happier metaphor.

Nor, indeed, did Cleghorn have it all his own way even amongst his peers. On Thursday, March 2, there was a meeting of the Employers' Association, a group whose membership overlapped that of the Board of Trade. The purpose of the meeting was to discuss the amalgamation issue. This was pretty generally agreed to be worth considering, but the chairman of the meeting, George Lang, a member of another of Berlin's prominent business families, and one of the few who joined W.H. Breithaupt when the battle heated up, also drew attention to the scuttlebutt, the rumours, and the unacceptable strategies of the name-changers that had plunged the city into its present crisis and called for an end to the campaign. As regards outside prejudices he stated categorically that his own tanning company had met with no objections to the name of Berlin. J. Kaufman, yet another famous local name, agreed that his company, too, had experienced little trouble selling Berlin goods. This was hardly the sort of information the name-changers wanted to hear, and Cleghorn was soon on his feet, spraying vitriol and uttering dire warnings at any manufacturer who supported such an offensive name, but he was interrupted by Lang, who coldly requested him to stop making threats. The pugnacious Scot, still muttering about how he would be proved right, sat down.

This meeting also saw a certain amount of backing down by the Cleghorn faction on what was turning out to be the crucial issue of how exactly the new name was to be chosen. They had, they claimed, acted out of the best of motives and had simply assumed that there was really no need to get an expression of opinion from the ratepayers, and that, yes, maybe they'd been a tiny bit hasty, but they'd asked lots and lots of people and they'd thought that that was sufficient. On the other hand, surely the seriousness of the situation justified being a little pushy. Everyone had now heard of the mysterious counter-petition (what did it say? who was behind it?), and every effort had to be made to combat it. To this end, a resolution was put to the meeting by Williams and Detweiler that all the manufacturers and professional men present add the weight of their names and those of their companies to the original petition to be presented to the City Council and the provincial Legislature. The motion passed when a standing vote came to be taken, but ominously there were several who remained in their seats. Clearly, in spite of Lang's plea for an end to the crisis, there were serious schisms at all levels in the city, and little hope for swift or painless solutions.

FIVE

The Tappert Skirmish

While the battle lines were being drawn in the press and at various meetings by the citizens of Berlin through the end of February and the first days of March, life for the lads of the 118th, who were kicking their heels while waiting for their battalion to be filled, went on its merry way. Training was barely basic, discipline was lax, movies were free, and hospitality generous, and there was always the chance of a decent punch-up on a Saturday night. The city's churches continued to line up to dine (though presumably not wine) the troops, so that at least once a week there was a free meal to be had. The speeches were boring, but the chicken was good, as was the service by the church ladies, who sometimes burst into song when the eating was over. On February 23, for example, St. Peter's Lutheran did the honours, though on this occasion the ladies visited the barracks with copious gifts of cakes, candy, cigarettes, and cigars. On March 2, it was the turn of Zion Evangelical (Breithaupt's church), and the next day St. Paul's Lutheran. It was all good public relations, particularly for the Lutheran churches which, with their large German congregations, many of whose members inevitably had family connections in the fatherland, were suspected of being responsible for much of the resistance to the war effort. Indeed, Rev. Boese of St. Paul's, in his address to the troops, talked at great length about the patriotic integrity of his church and congregation and why they still held some services in German (just for the older folk). The soldiers, of course, had too much integrity to be bought off by sweet talk and free meals. On the night before enjoying the St. Paul's hospitality they marched up King St. West to Carl Schultz's shoe repair shop and captured a large picture of "Kaiser Willie." They then went on into Waterloo, where they broke into Ritzer's tailor

76

shop and Doersam's bookstore where they stole more German memorabilia. Then it was back to Berlin, waving trophies and singing and shouting. At Gettas and Gettas they stopped for some sustenance, and when one of the other customers objected to their escapade he had a picture of the Kaiser smashed over his head and was chased out into the street. All good, clean fun as far as the *Telegraph* was concerned. The next night, George Ahrens found a soldier lying drunk in the gutter at the corner of King and Queen. He tried to help him but was set upon by other soldiers and ended up in hospital.

It should be noted here that it cannot have been the entire contingent of recruits, of whom there were by now about 400, that sparked these outrages. One particularly prominent group was the Machine Gun Section. They considered themselves a sort of elite corps of the 118th, but maybe they had already heard the grim statistic that the average life of a machine gunner in the trenches was about 22 minutes and were keen to do as much living as possible while there was still time. Then there were the likes of Sergeant Major Blood, who had figured out that their officers were a feeble lot, and that they could therefore be as lawless as they liked under the guise of patriotism. Of course other towns in Canada had their military riots, but in none were they as numerous or as ugly as they were in Berlin, whose unique history and ethnic composition were at the root of the conscription crisis. Here, in 1916, the image of the outlaw gang terrorizing the streets of a Wild West town while the sherrif cowers in his office was not so very far from the truth.

It was on Saturday night, March 4, that this group of military cowboys staged their most notorious escapade. At about 10 o'clock they were lounging about as usual outside Gettas and Gettas. It had been a slow evening. They'd had a few beers and tried some desultory recruiting, but there weren't enough "Yellowbacks" around for a good fight. What to do before drifting back to the barracks? Inevitably the name of Rev. C.R. Tappert came up. There had been talk of "having a word with him" on the night of the Concordia incident, but the idea had evaporated in the excitement of that night's events. Of course they'd visited Tappert's church before, though not exactly for purposes of worship. A couple of weeks earlier, Sunday, February 20, they'd marched into one of his services, as usual being conducted in German, disrupted his sermon, and when the recessional hymn was played at the end, broken into "God Save the King," and marched out. But this was a bit of a schoolboy prank, an amusing way of letting Tappert know that he wasn't welcome in Berlin — which, after all, was no more than what their colonel and, indeed, Sir Sam Hughes himself had said. Come to think of it, hadn't Tappert promised to leave the city by March 1? That was three days ago and he was still hanging around. Maybe a late night call on him at his home might help to speed him on his way. The idea was mentioned to Sergeant Major Blood, who allowed as how such a visit was long overdue, and that he'd be delighted to head the delegation. So off they set for the parsonage at 43 Alma St. It was to be Tappert's night.

Carl Reinhold Tappert was born in 1866 in Germany. He was trained for the ministry at the Kropp Seminary and when he was 22 had emigrated to the States, where he was ordained as a Lutheran pastor. At this time the Lutheran churches of Waterloo County, and indeed in the country as a whole, were still being supplied with pastors from the Synods in the States for the simple reason that there was no training institute for Lutheran clergy in Canada until the establishment of a seminary (the origin of Wilfrid Laurier University) in the town of Waterloo in 1911. Thus it was that in December 1912, Rev. C.R. Tappert came up from Meriden, Connecticut, as a candidate for the pastorate at St. Matthew's. A contemporary photograph shows an intelligent, clear-eyed man with a strong chin, a modest moustache, and a broad forehead sweeping up into slightly receding hair. It is a neat, slightly aristocratic face, perhaps a bit like Clifton Webb's when contemplating going down with the Titanic. The congregation was extremely impressed by his sermon on Sunday, December 8, and the next day unanimously asked him to become their minister. The future looked bright for Tappert. Not only was he to be in charge of the large and beautiful, new church that was about to be built at the corner of Benton and Church Streets, but he was also invited to join the faculty of the fledgling seminary in Waterloo. Early in 1913 the Tappert family was happily installed in the spacious parsonage on Alma St. It was fortunate that it was a good-sized house, as there were nine children.

The first sign of future problems occurred on September 28, 1914, at a meeting of the Ministers' Association on the subject of "War." During the debate Tappert publicly questioned the accuracy of the anti-German propaganda that was already beginning to inundate the country — which, even as early as this, was about as rash as questioning Holy Writ at the height of the Inquisition. He also said that he refused to contribute to the Patriotic Fund as a matter of conscience. The reaction, not only in Berlin but throughout the country, was instantaneous. He was rumoured to have been thrown in jail and transported to Ottawa. Toronto newspapers reported that he was in the habit of praying for the success of the Kaiser's army from his pulpit. Questions were asked in the House of Commons. The result of this gossip was the indignity of being summoned to appear before the Berlin police chief to explain himself.

But Tappert was not in the habit of backing down when it came to matters of principle — and one suspects that he was a man for whom most things were matters of principle. He defended himself forcefully before the police chief and then wrote an angry letter to A.P. Sherwood, the Chief Commissioner of the Canadian Police in Ottawa, demanding an apology, and an equally forceful one to the *News-Record*. Excerpts from the latter are useful for arriving at an understanding of Tappert's personality:

> On Sept the 28th., I was invited to attend "a regular meeting" of the Ministers' Association. "War" was the topic and, as a man who was raised and educated in Germany; has visited the old country in recent years and has always remained in contact with the trend of German thinking and feeling by a diligent study of German literature and frequent intercourse with representative German scholars; as a man who, living in an English speaking country for 27 years has attained standards of comparison and distance of observation so indispensable for forming a fair and unbiassed judgement, I expressed my views on certain phases in the popular presentation of this interesting subject "War." Almost all ministers present, although not agreeing with my views, received my remarks as one would expect of gentlemen. . . .
>
> The Germans are a liberty-loving nation and cherish independence of thinking and acting. I would rather sacrifice anything than bring up my family in a country where a man can be called to the police office for expressing his views at a Ministerial Association or upbraided by an official for having a conscience and acting according to its dictates.

He concluded by publishing Sherwood's letter of apology because "it will not only tend to silence the annoying reports respecting my person but at the same time serve to disengage the hearts of many good and loyal citizens from the depressing suspicion that the much vaunted liberty of this country be after all only an empty phrase."

One can well imagine the fury that such a letter must have engendered in many quarters (and embarrassment in others).

How could this man have the impudence to boast openly that he was a German and a diligent student of German "kultur"! And what about the heretical notion that the "Hun" was a lover of liberty, and the absolutely scurrilous insinuation that Canadians weren't! It was an offence against every decent instinct of a people whose minds were soggy with propaganda.

It is, of course, easy for us to see now what Tappert's intellectual and moral impulses were. He was essentially an academic who, as his letter makes clear, believed that dispassionate inquiry conducted by gentlemen will lead to the truth. Conversely, he had little respect for those who were not so guided. (It is interesting, perhaps ominous, that the subjects he taught at the Waterloo seminary were Dogmatics and Philosophy.) But he did not seem to have realized that there were very few people in Berlin at this time who were even remotely interested in "fair and unbiassed judgement," and that to attempt a rational discourse with them was like explaining the theory of relativity to a braying mob. (Mindless prejudice was not, of course, confined to Berlin or Canada. To take one of many possible examples, when Rev. Edward Lyttelton, headmaster of Eton, preached that the principles of Christian charity should be extended to Germany, he was accused of being either pro-German or a dangerous visionary, and forced to resign.) Tappert's fellow Lutheran preachers tended to keep their heads down in these dangerous times and, as we have seen, even flow with the prevailing madness, while waiting for better days. Tappert, who at worst can be accused of intellectual arrogance temperd by naivety, was constitutionally incapable of taking such a course. When he heard lies he had to stand up and refute them. This is not to say that the former were cowards. It is almost impossible in situations such as this to decide which is the ethical course of action. To be diplomatic or conciliatory encourages falsehood; to be openly confrontational is to endanger others — in Tappert's case his family and his congregation. The moral decision lies with the individual.

Throughout 1915, Tappert increasingly became a target of abuse. In March and April there was a celebrated exchange of letters between Tappert, Professor C.V. Reithdorf (like Dancey an itinerant firebrand on the propaganda circuit whose most impressive accomplishment, according to Patricia McKegney in *The Kaiser's Bust*, "was his ability to cause controversy and sow discord"), and W.H. Breithaupt. The correspondence began with Tappert correcting, in scholarly fashion, some facts about Germany's economy and political structure which Reithdorf had garbled for propaganda purposes in a recent lecture. Breithaupt briefly, and politely, got in on the act and received an equally polite reply from Tappert. Next came a vituperative riposte from Reithdorf, to which Tappert was actually in the process of replying when he was visited by two members of his Church Council, who requested him not to continue the argument. It was at the end of this letter that Tappert, with obvious sincerity, explained what his feelings were in this war between Germany and the Allies. He likened Germany to the mother that bore him, and America to the bride that he chose, and suggested that this was the situation for thousands of other Canadians.

> What will be the disposition of a good man toward his mother and his wife? Surely he will love them both. Therefore he will sincerely wish. . . . that they never get a-quarrelling. It will make him extremely unhappy if they do. It will cause him pangs of heart and conscience if he has to take sides, but whichever side he takes he will not be enthusiastic in throwing invectives at his mother just to show his new relatives how much he cares for his wife. . . . Sapienti sat.

To the many hundreds in Berlin who were in this position and no doubt feeling both bewildered and guilty, Tappert's words must have brought comfort. To many hundreds more they were close to treason.

But Tappert was saying no more than what had become the official German-Canadian line, expressed forcefully in an editorial in the *Berliner Journal*, the city's major German-language newspaper, on January 20, 1915. The naturalized German, it stated, has made a commitment to his adopted country, and *"eidt ist eidt,"* an oath is an oath, and is sacred. At the same time it is impossible for such people not to have feelings of attachment for the old country — as any good Canadian or Britisher would surely understand. The writer then rather neatly pushes the point home by quoting Sir Walter Scott's well-known lines: "Breathes there a man with soul so dead / Who never to himself hath said / This is my own, my native land" ("The Lay of the Last Minstrel") which might possibly have caused the likes of Cleghorn to pause for a moment or two before recovering with, "Ah, yes. . . . that! Well of course that's only if you're British. Doesn't apply to damned foreigners."

Throughout 1915 Tappert continued to demonstrate his integrity by publicly countering the slurs against "the mother that gave birth to me" and questioning the stories of German atrocities that were such a crucial part of the recruiting effort. He was, of course, perfectly correct to do so to the extent that most of these stories were fabrications, but this hardly endeared him to the patriotic Britisher. As the frustrations intensified in Berlin, and the angry suspicions about that elusive creature, the secret German sympathizer, increased, inevitably Tappert became more and more a focus of hatred. Most of the enemy kept well out of sight, but here was a target whose head and shoulders were squarely above the parapet. As we have seen, he was personally accused of being a subversive by Sam Hughes in the House of Commons, by Lochead and Dancey at public meetings, and in various letters to the press. Even an illiterate busybody at the local post office got in on the act. Tappert was in the habit of writing letters to acquaintances back at the Kropp Seminary. It was soon around town that he was sending secret messages to the Krupp Munitions Factory.

By the beginning of 1916, Tappert's position had become untenable. One suspects very strongly that his church wanted him to keep quiet, and probably Tappert himself realized that his congregation was suffering because of his notoriety. No doubt, too, the Lutheran Seminary, like most universities, was all for academic freedom for its faculty—within limits. Also his family was feeling the effects of his notoriety. His eldest daughter, Johanna, a teacher, was regularly escorted home by her principal in order to ensure her safety. On the morning after the sinking of the *Lusitania* she had been physically attacked in the school by a fellow teacher. She left the city in July 1915. Ruth, the second daughter, was a clerk at city hall, but was forced to resign in February 1916. It was reported in the papers that the Tappert boys refused to sing the national anthem at school because their father had ordered them not to do so—a false accusation according to the boys.

By February the personal and professional harrying had become too much, and Tappert tendered his resignation as pastor of St. Matthew's. It was accepted. His departure was generally assumed to be fixed for March 1, but in fact there was a confirmation service scheduled for March 5, and Tappert considered this too important an occasion to miss. Typically, he didn't disabuse anyone of the general assumption that he would be gone by the earlier date. As far as he was concerned it was nobody's business but his own and that of his parishioners. He would leave Berlin when he was ready to leave and not be seen scurrying off with his tail between his legs. The soldiers had other ideas.

Around 10:30, as Tappert was putting the finishing touches to his sermon for the confirmation service, there was a knock at the front door. Ruth opened it. In the dim light she saw a crowd of soldiers on the verandah, so she immediately slammed the door and locked it. The soldiers shouted that they simply wanted to have a friendly chat, but when this didn't seem to have the desired result, they smashed the window panels and unlocked the door. Tappert was at the phone calling for help, but he was pulled away and told to put his hat and coat on because he was going for a walk. Magdalena, his wife, then also tried to phone, but she was roughly shoved away, and the telephone wires were ripped from the wall. There was not much point anyway in trying to contact the police because the police were already there. Constables Sachs and Desmond had followed the mob at a safe distance, and once outside the parsonage had confined themselves to suggesting nervously that everyone should take it easy and then had watched the rest of the night's proceedings.

By this time there was a mob of about 50 people, some milling about in the hallway, others on the verandah jostling for a view and spilling down the steps and out onto Alma Street. Tappert, still uncowed, ordered the soldiers out of his house and began shoving at them, and he was immediately beaten up. One can imagine the pandemonium in the cramped space, what with the wrestling figures, the blows, Tappert's shouts, the insults of the soldiers, and the screams and cries of Mrs. Tappert and her children. Ruth struck out at the soldiers but only managed to bruise her hand. One son tried to find his father's rifle, but luckily it had been broken down for safety's sake and the parts stored in different places. Another son was knocked over the bannister. The battle, of course, was somewhat one-sided, though the soldiers later admitted that Tappert had put up a pretty good fight for someone in his fiftieth year. When it was over he had blood pouring down his face from scratches, a broken tooth, a blackened eye, and a cut on the back of his head.

But Tappert still refused to walk out of the house, so he was summarily picked up by his arms and legs and carried out. Outside, he was dropped onto the steps, and then asked if he would like more of that sort of treatment or would like to walk. He walked. Or rather he half stumbled and was half dragged along, with two men, Sergeant Major Blood and Private Schaefer, clutching his arms. And so the triumphal procession set off. The object, of course, was to make a public display of the victim in order to humiliate him. Down Alma to Benton they went, then a left turn at city hall, and so down King for three blocks to Yonge, passing on the way the many clubs and hotels of the city's centre, the Grand Central, the American, the Clarendon, the Grand Union, the Walper, the Brunswick, which were presumably just about now disgorging their customers. The noisy mob, and no doubt the onlookers, sang patriotic songs, and whooped and cheered lustily, while those actually supporting the captive cursed him heartily, or as Tappert said, "used very vile language." One wonders whether anyone watching the scene on that March night remembered that it was Easter.

At Yonge the cavalcade crossed the street and returned up King, pausing briefly outside the wrecked Concordia Club in order to invite the prisoner to contemplate the fate of all things German, and then on to Queen South and so to the barracks, where the intention was to throw him into the detention room for the night. At the barracks they were met by two junior officers, who were clearly intimidated by the situation, and dithered like people uncertain how to separate a vicious dog from its bone. At length Captain Fraser arrived, accompanied by an appalled Mayor Hett, and Tappert was finally surrendered. Hett hurried him to his surgery on King Street, where he cleaned him up and put stitches in his head, and then took him home.

There was an immediate inquiry. On Monday, Blood and Schaefer, the acknowledged ringleaders, were arraigned before Magistrate Weir on a charge of common assault. On the same day Lochead dashed off explanations to his superior officer in London, and the Adjutant General in Ottawa. To both he emphasized that he had repeatedly warned his men to leave Tappert alone or, as he said to the former, "appealed to the men to behave themselves," but alas Tappert's intransigence had proved too much for them. For Tappert he had no sympathy; his major concern was discipline, about which he was as keen as mustard. "While, therefore, I am not particularly worrying about Mr. Tappert, as he is not worthy of much consideration, I am nevertheless most anxious to maintain discipline." As for Blood, his behaviour was deeply disappointing. "He is an awfully good fellow but suffers his enthusiasm for the British cause to drown his good judgement." In the Police Court, Blood and Schaefer didn't contest the charges, were found guilty, and remanded for sentencing on the following Wednesday.

Tappert held his confirmation service on the Sunday, though perhaps it may not have been easy with a swollen lip, a bruised eye, a broken tooth, and a bandaged head. He later described the occasion in his *Reminiscences*:

> The church was filled, for I was to deliver my farewell sermon and also confirm a large class. Of what had taken place on the preceding night the church members had not yet heard. In the rear pews sat a number of soldiers. They had a message brought to me demanding that the service be conducted in English. Naturally I ignored their command. The members of the congregation who sat in the front pews were the first to notice my bandaged head, and the sound of sobbing grew in the church. They surmised what had happened, for this was not the first such exhibition of which these soldiers had been guilty.

According to one parishioner, "his last confirmation service is graven indelibly upon the memory of a congregation that will ever hold him in grateful remembrance as the builder of her beautiful church, as a scholarly preacher and a cultured Christian gentleman." After the service it was back to Alma Street to pack up in readiness for departure three days later.

On Wednesday morning, Magistrate Weir's courtroom was packed with soldiers and civilians. Weir gave the two culprits a brief tongue-lashing, in which he told them that soldiers should consider themselves as responsible for law and order as the police, which was unintentionally ironic, and asked them whether 50 against one was their definition of British fair play. And at the end of the lecture he sternly put them on suspended sentences. "Those present expressed themselves as being heartily in favour of the manner in which Magistrate Weir disposed of the case." The partisan cheers, the weak reprimand, and the more or less non-existent sentence all boded ill for the future, but it was some words that Weir addressed specifically to Blood that were particularly chilling. "Rumours have come to me that you are the leader of a certain section of men who have planned to call upon other citizens of both this city and of Waterloo and subject them to treatment similar to that received by the Rev. Mr. Tappert." One surmises that public knowledge of Blood's hit list, plus the evident inability of the military authorities to control their men, had a significant effect on the events of the next months.

On the afternoon of the same day that Blood and Schaefer were being punished, Tappert and his family quietly left Berlin on the 2:32 for Buffalo. There were few people at the station to see them leave.

SIX

Defeat at Queen's Park

The two campaigns, to change the name and to raise a battalion, had, by April 1916, become fatefully intertwined. As Captain Fraser rather menacingly, but accurately, told his audience at the Star Theatre, "It is needless for me to say that the interests of Berlin are bound up in the fortunes of the 118th Battalion." And this was so on both a symbolic and a practical level. On the symbolic level, though all parties were agreed that recruitment was an absolute priority, one faction argued that this was the best way to prove Berlin's patriotism no matter what the city was called, while the other faction was touchingly convinced that changing the name would somehow solve the recruiting and most other problems. On the practical level, the behaviour of the military on the streets provoked incidents that only served to harden attitudes and keep the animosity flowing between soldier and citizen.

And such "incidents" certainly continued unabated. On Saturday, March 11, for example, two civilians were accused by passing soldiers of making derogatory remarks and were immediately arrested. On Monday they were fined $60.00 by Weir. On Tuesday, March 14, a soldier accused three civilians of assaulting him. The charge was denied, but they too went before Weir. On March 29, Lochead had to write a letter full of the most abject apologies to Julius Luft of 28 Spring Street because soldiers had broken into his house and the house of one of his neighbours, smashed property, and generally "behaved themselves in an unbecoming manner." He assured Luft that "they will never again attempt to molest anyone. . . . without proper authority (sic)," and asked to be sent the bill. One remembers that it was only three weeks earlier, during the Tappert inquiry, that Lochead had given the citizens of Berlin identical assurances about his troops' behaviour. The incident underlines, if any underlining is needed, how ineffectual his authority had become.

On Friday, March 31, a certain Harry Kreitzer was in Police Court charged with interfering with recruiting. He was apparently a member of the "notorious" Lyric Club, which had been raided on December 13, 1915, by Kreitzer's military namesake, and which was still peddling a seditious pamphlet to potential recruits. It is perhaps significant that the pamphlet was not so much pro-German as "socialistic in its sentiments." Weir gave him a suspended sentence. But perhaps the fracas that occurred on Saturday, April 15, best summarizes the total lack of understanding displayed by the military and also illustrates that they were by no means dealing with a cowed populace. As reported by the *News-Record*, Private Joe Yanchus was recruiting with a couple of buddies when they came across Herman Schnarr. They asked him why he wasn't in uniform, but "the accused refused to answer, merely laughing and sneering at the questioners." Yanchus threatened to "knock his block off," and grabbed him, at which point Schnarr socked Yanchus on the nose. Schnarr was then worked over, and eventually, with the help of an officer was taken to the recruiting offices. In court on the following Monday morning, A.B. McBride, defending Schnarr, questioned Captain Lockhart about the army's *modus operandi*.

McBride: Why do you use these rough tactics to get men?
Lockhart: We don't use rough tactics at all. The fault lies with the civilians who wont be civil to the recruiters.
McBride: Do you authorize your recruiters to threaten to knock the block off anyone not enlisting?
Lockhart: Certainly not! My men conduct themeslves like gentlemen, and if it were not for sneering, impudent fellows like the accused, who wont answer a civil question there would be no trouble at all.

It all sounded depressingly familiar (as McBride wearily stated, "We have these fights every night in Waterloo") though just occasionally there might be a flash of comedy. Schnarr stated that he hadn't enlisted because he had old and feeble parents, and seven sisters, one of whom suffered "with nervous perspiration." "Nervous prostration you mean," said Weir. "Yes! that's it," said the accused (laughter in court).

But all these altercations were mere pinpricks, petty skirmishes in a much larger and more serious campaign that occupied the energies of Berlin from March 21 to April 11. The results of recruiting in the previous three or four months had been pathetic. It seemed as though everything possible had been done to raise troops, short of sowing dragon's teeth on the sidewalks, but the battalion still needed 700 men. What was worse, a rumour was circulating that the battalion was going to be shipped off to London in May, and that if it was not at full strength the men would simply be dispersed to other units. Thus a time pressure was now added to those of civic honour and dignity. But 700 men was a tall order, considering the current recruiting record. What was needed was a massive campaign to get men into uniform, a crash course that would involve every organization, every factory, every business, and every club; a campaign that would capture the hearts and minds of every citizen of Berlin. Such a blitz could not be sustained over a long period of time. For fullest effect it would have to be swift and focussed, say, over a three-week period. Seven hundred men in three weeks! It had a bold, not to say heroic, ring to it. Seven hundred men in three weeks! Surely with a supreme effort it could be achieved.

The 700 Men In Three Weeks campaign was officially launched on Tuesday, March 21. Great streamers were hung across King Street proclaiming the heady slogan, the sides of the street cars were similarly embellished, and all the store windows were draped with posters and flags. A long yellow line was painted on the sidewalk (a forerunner of the modern United Appeal thermometer), and each day the troops formed up along it, and it was extended as the recruits came in. Further up the street, a depressingly long way up, a yellow arrow indicated how far the line had to reach. Every day for three weeks the newspapers carried articles on their front pages, exhorting, cajoling, scolding, and praising the young men of the city, and every day, not just on Saturdays, there were speeches and meetings on street corners and in the theatres, and the military band marched hither and yon, instilling martial sentiments in everyone's breasts.

And lest the potential recruit should think that he might find refuge from this bombardment during the day, the city's work spaces were also systematically invaded. A list of all the 100 or more substantial factories and businesses was drawn up, and each was visited by detachments of troops and officers and bands. The machinery was stopped and tools and pens were laid down, and the band played and the men sang and cheered, and speeches were made right there on the shop floor or amongst the clerk's desk by scarred veterans and civic bigwigs and factory bosses — though one hazards the guess that a few of the latter might have harboured the secret hope that their workers wouldn't take any notice. Still, they had to be perceived to be doing their duty.

Then there were the "Get A Man" cards. These could be picked up at the recruiting office or the theatres or at a number of shops. They were blank forms on which one simply had to fill out the name and address of any man one thought should be wearing the King's uniform, and then slip them to a member of the military. The recruiting teams did the rest. The cards were said to have been a great help in winkling out the bashful. It is not known whether they were used to settle old scores. Cleghorn, as chairman of the Recruiting Committee, also wanted the names of those who refused to enlist posted in public places, but this does not appear to have been done.

The inaugural meeting was at the Grand Theatre. Speeches and songs and, as a special treat, Baby Clarice Ostell, aged 8, dressed in a cute little khaki suit, singing "Tommy Atkins," got things off to a fine start. The campaign would involve saturation coverage, though the organizers insisted, making a misplaced stab at public relations, that the coverage would not be offensive. "We are going into this campaign," said Dr. Honsberger, "with 100 picked men from the battalion who will interview in the factories, banks, stores and offices. They will stop you on the streets perhaps a dozen times a day. Don't resent it for they will be courteous." And Captain Routley added,

> We are going to get 700 men by diplomacy. There will be no rough stuff unless it is started by the civilians, and then, well you know the boys of the 118th! We are going to be as persistent as an agent for a sewing machine who calls again and again until you buy it to get rid of him. That is the system we are going to adopt to get men for the Battalion. We will keep after them until they join to get rid of us.

With tactics so insensitive and so totally devoid of common sense, the campaign was obviously doomed from the start, though hopes were high in the first few days. The *News-Record*, for example, pulled out all the stops of its euphonium in claiming "that the desired result will be attained there is little doubt" and mystically reported that it could already hear "the tramp, tramp, tramp of Berlin's best manhood" marching to the recruiting office. But ominous signs were already there. An encouraging 77 men signed up on the first two days, but alas, their tramp, tramp, tramp, turned out to be more of a plod, plod, plod as half of them were rejected as medically unfit due to flat feet and other ailments. Furthermore, anyone who had bothered to work it out would have seen that a rate of 20 recruits a day (making the unlikely assumption that such a rate would be maintained) would only bring in slightly more than half the required number.

Within a week the initial optimism was being replaced by sorry stories of the difficulties the recruiters were encountering. A depressingly familiar situation in the factories was that as the military band marched in at one door the workers had a habit of slipping out of another, only to return once the coast was clear. And the excuses that were being put forward! "Mother wont let me." "I'm not ready yet." "There's no money in it." It was all so pathetic and contemptible. At one house the mother who opened the door to the soldiers stated that the young man they desired to see was not at home, and that there were no other men of eligible age there. "After taking their departure the soldiers spied three hopefuls, all of military age, in company with the aforesaid 'lady,' peeping from a top storey window." Another woman was rather more outspoken. She would, she said, "sooner shoot her son in the backyard than have him fight the enemy." These incidents are a reminder of the one World War I song that was never heard at the recruiting rallies: "I Didn't Raise My Boy To Be A Soldier." Worst of all were those who gave false names and addresses, thereby sending the follow-up squads on wild goose chases. This tactic infuriated even the usually mild *News-Record.*

> By this dirty lie they not only damn their own souls (if they ever had any) and self confess themselves the most despicable and mean of God's creatures, but also they throw a barrier in the way of the recruiting and by so doing are committing the criminal offence of INTERFERING WITH RECRUITING which offence IS PUNISHABLE BY A TERM OF TWO YEARS IMPRISONMENT.

Maybe the message was inserted at the insistence of the Recruiting Committee. It certainly has Cleghorn's delicate touch.

Nor should class resentments be forgotten as a reason why some refused to enlist. At one packed meeting at the Grand Theatre, while Major Boehm was making an impassioned pitch, "a voice from somewhere in the front seats rang out across the building: 'I won't go until some of the rich men's sons enlist. Let some of the Langs, Krugs and Breithaupts get into khaki for overseas service' (cheers)." The theme was picked up again by a featured speaker later in the campaign, but with much more vitriol.

> And our wealthy citizens! What about them? Some are true I know and have played their part nobly, but there are others — big, bloated parasites, some of whom came here a few years ago with the seats out of their trousers and the toes out of their boots, illiterate, ignorant immigrants — and their wives as illiterate as themselves. Today they are reckoned among the princes of fortune, their sons in sabled furs drive their autos, or find their way back to the States in order, we are told, to COMPLETE THEIR EDUCATION. After the war has ended these contemptible creatures will return to Berlin and the society columns will ring out the announcement of the fact "that their education being now complete Messrs So and So have returned to the city." These are the specimens, ladies and gentlemen, who refuse to take up arms, and who prefer that others shall fight their battles. They are not wanted in Berlin!

One wonders whether the organizers of the campaign felt entirely comfortable with this slightly Bolshevik approach, but the speaker seems to have been a law unto himself. It was Granville Blood.

As the great campaign wound down to its unsuccessful conclusion, the recruits dribbling in now at only two or three a day, the tone of speeches and articles lapsed more and more into insult and vituperation, but all to no avail. The young men of Berlin and North Waterloo were "selfish, ignorant curs," "social pariahs," "miserable creatures," and "soulless degenerates." When the battle is perceived to be lost, what is there left to ease the feelings but curses. In its short, muted editorial of Wednesday, April 12, the *News-Record* tried to put a brave face on the failure. "Effective work has been done in many directions," it said fuzzily, and certainly "the work of soliciting men will be continued up to the hour of departure." But one senses that hopes were not high. Three or four hundred men were still needed, and time was getting desperately short.

At the same time as the 700 Men In Three Weeks campaign was being waged, the name-change issue was being assiduously promoted, with the idea of amalgamation with Waterloo at this point very much in the forefront of everyone's mind. Both places had struck Amalgamation Committees, Berlin's consisting of

Mayor Hett; J.M. Scully, the city auditor; J.C. Breithaupt, another of the Breithaupt brothers and chairman of the Water Commission; George Lippert, chairman of the Light Commission; and W.D. Euler, former mayor and future M.P.P. The committee is interesting for the absence of any members of the Cleghorn faction. As has been noted, Hett was at the very least ambiguous about changing the name, as, one may guess, was Breithaupt; Scully later came out against such a move; and Euler came into his own the following year when he bravely and victoriously led the fight against the rabid Britishers. (Interestingly enough he was also a former lawn-bowling teammate of Cleghorn's, but now he was running on a different political bias.) That these men led the amalgamation talks suggests that the climate in Berlin now was such that even those who did not really believe in changing the name were not prepared to risk outright opposition, were maybe fatalistic about the final outcome, and saw amalgamation as a sort of second-best option.

On the evening of Thursday, March 16, Mayor Hilliard and his Waterloo delegation travelled down King Street to meet with their Berlin counterparts in Hett's office. Everything seems to have been covered at this initial meeting, from sewage systems, to garbage, to post offices, to cemeteries, to county taxes, mill rates, public utilities, council representation, and whether water mains were ten inches or eight inches in diameter. At the end of it all Mayor Hilliard cautiously suggested that there were still several points that needed to be given more consideration. After all, amalgamation had been bobbing around for a long time, and on each occasion it had slipped away due to some misunderstanding or other. And then, too, perhaps they should all await the result of the petition to change Berlin's name that was going to be presented to the Special Bills Committee at Queen's Park sometime in April. Meanwhile he could say quite confidently that "on general principles I think we are all agreed that the proposal is good. We see no irremovable difficulties." And, oh yes, perhaps he should reiterate that of course Waterloo would be the name of the new city. These preliminary wedding negotiations have a curious feel to them right from the start. It is as though a large, unhappy groom is making overtures to a much smaller, rather wary bride, who is becoming evasive about the dowry and who wants the union to be blessed with her name.

But perhaps Hilliard was right to underline this last point, because by now the game of suggesting new names for Berlin had become as popular as buying lottery tickets is today. A few days earlier the City Council had confirmed that it would offer $300 for the best name, and what had already been a steady stream of suggestions had now become a flood. Nor was this interest confined by any means to Berlin. From across Canada the letters came pouring in. Then, as the fame of the contest grew, suggestions started coming from abroad, from the States and New Zealand and Mexico. There was one estimation that 10,000 letters arrived, containing 30,000 names. This may have been an exaggeration, but there were certainly enough for Hett to ask despairingly what on earth his office was going to do with them all.

And what names they were. One of the well-known facts of this story is that the six names initially put forward by the Berlin City Council were so dreadful that they provoked universal derision and had to be dropped. What is less well known is that the names that were eliminated were as bad if not worse. There was Boroughland and Boroughlion, Berylyn, Beaverlyn, and Berlouberg. There was Hydro City, which was something of a frontrunner, and several variants like Hydrolite, and Hydropolis, and Hydrolia, though someone objected that it all sounded too much like hydrophobia. There was Waterlin, because it combined Waterloo and Berlin, and the perhaps disingenuous Britton, because it combined British and Teuton. There was a slew of Indian names such as Wakasha, Kanateio, Tecumseh, Dynandah, and Mohawk City. There was Awatto, because it was Ottawa backwards, and Canawa, because it was half Canada and half Ottawa. There was Alert City because the people were alert, and Thrift City because the people were thrifty, and Mines City or City of Mines, because 80 percent of the people owned their own homes and could say, "mine's home." And there was the inevitable joker, like the man who suggested, though not quite getting it right, the record-breaking name of the Welsh town, Llanfairpwllgwyngyllgogerychwyrndrobwylllantysibogogo-goon. Not surprisingly the letter was signed "Taffy." And there continued to be a smattering of letters that urged the retention of Berlin.

At the weekly meeting of City Council of Monday, March 20, there was a report from the Amalgamation Committee, a remarkably familiar discussion about escalating hospital costs, and queries about whether the provincial government had set a date for hearing the petition to change the name. This business was soon disposed of, and the meeting got down to the crucial issue that was clearly occupying everyone's mind: the actual process that would be employed for choosing the new name. The old arguments were once again recycled, with the Board of Traders arrogantly insisting that there was no need to consult the general public on the matter, and Hett doggedly insisting that he could not agree to any proposal which would deprive the ratepayers of a say in the matter. There were hidden agendas on both sides, and both pertained to the unreliability of plebiscites.

The debate on this issue slowly became more impassioned. Suddenly Hahn rose and demanded point blank that Hett state whether or not he was himself in favour of changing the name. The Mayor, caught slightly off balance, ruled the question out of order, which brought on a (probably artificial) fit of astonishment from his antagonist.

> I asked you a fair question, and here you are, the Mayor, refusing to declare yourself on the question of changing the name of the city. Think of it, gentlemen! I never saw anything like it! Goodness gracious, what do you think of it! The Mayor of this city refuses to say whether or not he is favour of changing the city's name!

The pseudo-indignation was an obvious attempt to embarrass the mayor, or worse, and Gross quickly tried to bring the discussion back to the voting process, but he was shouted down with cries of "Speak to the question!" Hett, however, kept stonewalling with out-of-order rulings and, for this meeting at least, was able to steer attention away from his personal beliefs. But it had been an unpleasant episode, and he must have wondered how the atmosphere of Council could have changed so radically from the camaraderie of just three months earlier. As he ruefully, and perhaps a little wearily, remarked at another point in the discussion, "I get the blame for a great many things these days." It was nothing to the battering that he would shortly take.

The meeting eventually left the contentious issue more or less hanging in the air. It was vaguely agreed that a committee, headed by Cleghorn and Hallman, should be appointed to help sort out the names being suggested, but how these names were to be reduced to a votable number, let alone the crucial matter of who should be included in the voting for the final name, well perhaps this could be taken up again at the meeting of Monday, April 3. It had been an exhausting session, but Hett did manage one small victory. Millar, the city clerk, was voted extra help to cope with his increased mail load.

And the letters continued to pour in. Three hundred a day. Two thousand a week. They came in big envelopes and little envelopes, in white, yellow, pink, brown and blue envelopes, as writers from across the continent twisted their imaginations into excruciating knots in attempts to win first prize in Name That City. There were the barmy portmanteau names like Ingirescot (presumably Wales couldn't be fitted in) and MaryGeo or possibly GeoMary (in honour of the king and queen) and Brockwack (Wackett was some sort of local hero). There was Dry Town (perhaps from a hopeful temperance competitor) and DeBus City (maybe from someone who liked getting his hair cut). Someone with a tenuous grasp of both history and logic proposed Cromwell because he was knighted by Elizabeth in 1669 and never lost a battle, while others with equally tenuous grasps of nomenclature tried Vespugo and Magnocephauls. There was Art City and Grand City and Empire City and Rex City and Lion City and Main City and Shamrock City and Emporium and New Berlington. Inevitably there was Adanac. From Prince Edward Island came a 1,000-word telegram arguing for Astrea. It cost the sender $7.00, and cheap at the price if he'd won. Perhaps more puzzling was the suggestion from Garson, Manitoba, that the name be Leap Year, not simply because it was, but because all the young ladies would like to get married there so that they could say that they were married in Leap Year. And the jokers continued to have a field day with suggestions like Rottend-kaiserdam, Williamsblunder, and Johnbullsberg.

Of course there was more to it than simply the excitement of a countrywide game show. As the promoters of the contest were well aware, the very fact of getting everyone involved in choosing a new name meant that psychologically everyone assumed that a new name was to be chosen, even before Queen's Park, and perhaps local voters, expressed their opinions. It was a clever presumptive tactic, one that made the task of those opposed to any change at all, of whom there was clearly a large number (almost certainly the silent majority) all the harder.

April 3 and 4 were important days for the proponents of the name change. On Monday evening the City Council was once again going to try to thrash out the manner in which the new name was to be chosen; and on Tuesday morning most of the members were off to Toronto, for this was the day that the Special Bills Committee would consider, and presumbly approve, the petition to change the name. Yet if there was an element of carts before horses in this ordering of events it was more apparent than real. After all, there could be little doubt that the Queen's Park committee would agree to such an impeccably patriotic request supported, as it was, by an overwhelming majority of the city's government, and anyway it could really do no harm to demonstrate that the whole voting mechanism for changing the name was set and ready to go.

Not that the Monday evening meeting really resolved that much. Cleghorn and Hallman, of course, led off with their proposal that their own committee should choose the name. Exhibiting an aristocratic disdain for democratic processes, they tried to dismiss the competence of the general public in a matter of such great importance, argued that they were the ones who had done all the work in the campaign and were therefore the only ones with the necessary expertise to make informed choices, and suggested that hardly anyone would come out to vote even if they were given the opportunity to do so. Of course they didn't mention that this continuing attempt to hijack the decision-making process was due to the fear that a public vote might not produce the desired result. Hett, as before, opposed these arguments, and he was supported by Gross, Reid, and Gallagher — perhaps the men most in touch with the working-class voters. The indomitable Gross inquired whether Berlin should not be one of the names on the final list, and almost in unison Cleghorn and Hallman shouted "No!" When he further asked whether there had been suggestions that the name be retained, Hallman dismissively stated that there were one or two but that they weren't worth bothering with. As it was public knowledge that there was a "counter-petition" bearing nearly 1,000 signatures, one assumes that Hallman was merely being dishonest. Certainly Gross persisted in pointing out that the omission of Berlin would effectively disenfranchise many people, at which point the meeting once again got fractious, and it was almost with relief that they heard Alderman Schnarr's plaintive reminder about a matter that seemed to have been forgotten in all the sound and fury. What about amalgamation with Waterloo? But no one was interested in amalgamation at this juncture, and for the time being at least it was relegated to a back burner.

In the end it was agreed that a Committee of Ninety-Nine should be empowered to make a short list of six names (taken from a "long" list prepared by the Cleghorn/Hallman committee's perusal of *all* the suggestions), to be submitted to City Council which would then decide, at some later date, how the final selection should be made. This vast, unwieldy committee was to be composed of representatives from a number of public bodies such as the Public School Board (10), the Separate School Board (6), the Library Board (4), the Ministerial Association (6), the Roman Catholic Fathers (2), and so on. The Committee looked ungainly, but it probably represented a small tactical victory for the Cleghorn faction. In the first place it was heavily weighted in their favour, because many of the "public bodies" had overlapping interests and, indeed, identical memberships. Thus the City Council (16), the Board of Trade (10), the Manufacturers (5), the Merchants (5), and the Commercial Travellers (5), mustered very nearly half the votes of the committee, and the only body that might possibly be expected to represent any sort of an opposition was the Trades and Labour Council (10). Secondly, when the matter of the final choice arose again, it could be plausibly argued that such an enormous committee was clearly representative of the city as a whole and that therefore a public vote was totally unnecessary. It was probably as neat a solution as could be expected in the circumstances, even if it wasn't as satisfactory as ramming the whole thing through without all this pseudo-democratic fuss and bother. Meanwhile there were one or two hurdles to negotiate, one of the smaller ones being the meeting with the Private Bills Committee the next day.

The G.T.R. station on Victoria was an interesting spot on Tuesday morning as the petitioners gathered to catch the early train to Toronto. On the platform was the "official" delegation, consisting of Hett and Aldermen Hallman, Hessenauer, Rudell, Master, Cleghorn, Schnarr, and Ferguson; Millar, the city clerk, and Sims, the city solicitor; plus loyal supporters such as Sam Williams, Dr. Honsberger, George DeBus, and Alan Eby. Nearby was a second, much smaller group, which no doubt received many a dirty look from the first. This was the group that was carrying the counter-petition. It was composed of W.H. Breithaupt, J.M. Scully the city auditor, H.M. Bowman, and A.B. McBride, the Waterloo attorney who was in the habit of defending Berlin citizens when they ran afoul of military recruiters.

Once in Toronto the two groups made their separate ways to Queen's Park, but finally and uncomfortably came face to face in the room being used that morning by the Private Bills Committee. And now, one imagines, sat expectation in the air. The official delegation, "proud of their numbers and secure in soul" were certainly full of confidence, as well they might be. Not only were they secure in the righteousness of their cause, but for the past few days Williams, who had many contacts in government circles, had been assiduously lobbying committee members, both Liberal and Conservative, and had received firm promises of support from 33 of them. In a committee that would number around 50 this would be more than enough to ensure a success-ful passage for their petition. It had been scheduled to come before the committee at 10:30, but the two previous bills had taken longer to dispose of than anticipated and it wasn't until a little after 11:00 a.m. that the Honourable H.B. Lucas, the attor-ney-general, called for Bill 44, adding the enigmatic aside, "Ah, the Berlin bill. This shouldn't take long to dispose of."

C.H. Mills, the Conservative M.P.P. for Waterloo North, opened the proceedings with studied impartiality by introducing the issue and the two delegations. And here it is important to note that while the official petition was asking permission for Berlin to change its name, the counter-petition was simply requesting that such a change be put to a public vote. Theoreti-cally, then, the issue was only concerned with process. In other words, the counter-petitioners appear to have conceded that some sort of an election process would have to occur, but that if they could only get all the ratepayers of Berlin involved in the vote there might still be a chance of somehow retaining their city's name.

Solicitor Sims led off for the City Council. He explained the chaotic situation in Berlin, no doubt in lurid terms, argued for the absolute necessity for a change of name, and flourished a list of signatures, which had grown to 1,170 names of loyal citizens who demanded such a change. McBride, in reply, flourished his own list of 900 names and accused the opposition of padding their own list. Fifty percent of the names, he said, were without votes, were non-residents or minors, and as for the much vaunted list of businesses said to be in favour of the change, well he had some of them on his own list as well. The provincial politicians seemed strangely restless through all this, and the questions when they came were a little disturbing. Various honourable members such as Thomas Crawford and George Gooderham wondered why the vote wasn't to be submitted to the people, and Sims had to jump in with dire predictions of race riots if the wretched city was subjected to such a demo-cratic procedure. Unfortunately this argument didn't have the desired effect; it was agreed that such a vote might well have extremely unpleasant consequences, and that therefore perhaps it should be shelved until after the war.

Clearly there was something wrong. The meeting was definitely not moving in the direction that the name-changers had expected or, indeed, been promised. In an attempt to save the situation the request was made that Williams be allowed to address the committee. His rumbling rhetoric had thrilled many a recruiting meeting back in Berlin, and now was the time to put it to even better use. Besides, he had a certain clout amongst the committee members and, as far as he was concerned, a few favours to call in. "There is not a man on the City Council," he told the committee, conveniently forgetting Gross and Reid, "on whom the name of Berlin does not grate, and to whose nose it does not smell obnoxious and distasteful." As for those 900 on the other petition, "Well, if those 900 would get into khaki our battalion would be filled (applause and cheers)." Warming to his theme now, he used McBride's tactic of questioning the eligibility of the names on the enemy petition. "Thirty five per cent of those people on their petition are foreigners," he cried, but was then rather thrown off balance by a voice that asked "What do you mean by foreign?" "Foreign-born people," replied Williams. "Naturalized?" asked the insistent voice. By now the distracted Williams could only stutter, but he knew he would be all right when he got to his peroration. It was a good one. On patriotism. And he was just about to get going on it when, of all the extraordinary things, here was Lucas asking the committee if there were any more questions. Before he'd even finished. The next few seconds went by so fast that it was all over before anyone realized it. "All those in favour of Bill 44," asked Lucas. There were a few mumbles and a couple of raised hands. "The bill is lost." Both delegates sat in stunned silence. Berlin was not going to lose its name after all.

SEVEN

Victory at Queen's Park

It was probably the Breithaupt group that was initially the more astounded. The decision was beyond their wildest dreams; indeed, it was one that they hadn't even requested. In the corridor outside the committee room one reporter said that they looked like small boys standing longingly under a peach tree suddenly being hit on the head by an enormous peach. As for the jingoists, the initial shock quickly turned to fury. The traitorous Scully was surrounded by irate aldermen, and one of them (one guesses either Hallman or Cleghorn) gave vent to his fury. The Toronto *Telegram* description, slightly sanitized for family consumption, catches the flavour of the scene: "'You'll get out, blank you,' shouted one of the aldermen. 'Perhaps I will and perhaps I won't,' said Mr. Scully. 'You'll get out. I'll see that you're fired, and fired mighty quick too,' roared the alderman." On the other side of the corridor Breithaupt, Bowman, and McBride had been backed up against the wall and were receiving similar treatment.

> You're a lot of blank Germans, that's what you are. We'll show you whether you can lobby a committee and have a bill thrown out. We'll drive you out of town, that's what we'll do to you. Huh! You people loyal? Why, the elements take your hides, you don't know what loyalty is.

But what had gone wrong? Verbally assaulting Breithaupt and his crew for being "Hun" lovers, for playing dirty pool, for having the temerity to lobby provincial politicians — which was, after all, no more than Williams had been doing — was a reflex action to the immediate debacle, but were the actions of these gentlemen the only reason why 33 votes had quietly vanished

100

like an early morning mist? Clearly more sinister and more pow-erful forces had been secretly at work. Speculation about what these forces were began almost immediately. The *Telegraph* reported one political tea-leaf reader as declaring that it had something to do with byzantine backroom deals connected with the prohibition campaign then in progress. He'd observed a committee member studying the names on the official petition and heard him say, "This seems to be a sort of temperance peti-tion," causing his friends to snicker. Another noticed that the most vocal opposition came from the Toronto M.P.P.'s, and that it was probably an attempt to undermine Berlin industry by rival interests in the provincial capital.

But fingers were more seriously pointed at C.H. Mills. It was remembered that when he introduced the rival delegations he was studiously impartial, which was clearly not the democratic way to proceed. He should have come out strongly in favour of the elected council of the largest city in his constituency. Why didn't he? In such a situation impartiality was tantamount to opposition. Obviously he was secretly against the name change and, it was soon put about, had himself lobbied the committee and, according to one supporter of the counter-petition, "had things pretty well fixed." But did Mills have sufficient clout for this sort of power-broking? Maybe there was somebody even bigger lurking in the shadows of the throne itself. Winkling out guilt at the very top, which might today be known as the Water-gate Syndrome, has always been popular; it adds a touch more frisson to the scandal and, in cases such as this one, helps to jus-tify defeat.

In fact there was a prime candidate for the role of Mr. Big, none other than Sir Adam Beck. Born in Baden and educated in Galt, Beck had many friends in Berlin. Well of course he did. The man was himself of German extraction. And as Minister without Portfolio in the Hearst government and long-time chair-man of the Hydro-Electric Power Commission he was a figure of considerable influence. And wasn't Lucas one of his fellow com-missioners? The plot was as plain as the nose on your face. Sam Williams later went public with the inside story in a letter to the *News-Record*—though unfortunately his information was sec-ond-, possibly third-hand. According to Williams, there had been a meeting at the Walper House (or maybe it was Toronto's Walker House; no one seemed to be quite sure) attended by Sir Adam Beck, Scully, Mills, McBride, and eight members of the Private Bills Committee, and it was here that the whole wretched conspiracy was hatched. Indeed, Williams was able to quote McBride's very own words on the matter:

> After a few preliminaries the matter was arranged as to how it (the Bill) was to be handled. It was the easiest case I ever had, and the easiest money I ever earned in my life, and I repeat you would not have had a ghost of chance, no matter how many names you had on your petition in favour of the Bill.

So that explained it all. Except that a couple of days later there was a terse reply from Scully stating that although "the name and reputation of the Hon. Sir Adam Beck stand so far above those of some of our citizens who assail him that he needs no help from me to defend him," he would like to point out that he had never at any time or in any circumstances met with Beck at the Walper House — or the Walker House. And the next day McBride chipped in with the assertion that,

> if some mysterious and nefarious plot was hatched against King George incidentally, and Mr. S.J. Williams particularly, in some dark, subterranean vault or cavern under The Walker House, by the Kaiser with Sir Adam Beck, C.H. Mills and J.M. Scully as chief myrmidons I plead an alibi. I was not there and know nothing whatever about the matter.

He also suggested that he was not inclined to be drawn into a newspaper controversy about himself personally or the easy money he was said to have earned, though one suspects that he may have privately threatened legal action because the next day Williams apologized for his assertions and withdrew them.

Whatever the truth of the matter, the reaction of the petitioners (after their initial disbelief and fury) was mixed. Some aldermen threatened to resign. Others, Hett for example, took a philosophical view of the situation, and one suspects that the philosophy was tinged with delight. From solicitor Sims there were veiled warnings of the on-their-own-heads-be-it variety. But the Jacobin wing of the City Council and their supporters angrily swore that they would fight Teutonic perfidy to the last.

The last-named group had to do something, for their fortunes at this juncture were at a low ebb. Not only had they sustained a major defeat before the Private Bills Committee, but the 700 Men In Three Weeks campaign was in the process of petering out, not with the hoped-for bang, but with a deplorable whimper. As has been recounted, every avenue of persuasion had been explored in that campaign, but with increasingly unsatisfactory results. In its last days the old tactic was employed of making wounded veterans, now beginning to return from the front in increasing numbers, the focus of recruiting rallies. On April 3, for example, Corporal Mitchell was paraded through the streets, and had a $5.00 gold piece pressed into his hand by the Daughters of the Empire, and a few days later Sergeant Davis was given a similar welcome. However, the fact that the former had to receive his gold piece with his one remaining hand, and the latter had to be supported because shrapnel in his neck had paralyzed him, did nothing to persuade potential recruits.

And the day before the end of the campaign there was the case of the patriotic collie. Not only did it attach itself to the 118th Battalion as back-up to the official mascot, "Czar," a Russian wolfhound, but it was also observed chasing after another dog, appropriately enough a dachshund. "Ye Gods," said the *News-Record*," what are the young fellows of Berlin coming to when it needs the stray dogs of the city to show them their duty to their country!" But the canine symbolism didn't help. There was only one recruit that day. Apart from the dog.

It took the name-change forces only six days to regroup and start their counter-offensive. On Monday evening, April 11, some 60 people gathered at the Nobby Club for the purpose of creating a brand new organization whose express aim would be to "promote British sentiment in the community" and, more urgently, to get the name-change issue back to Queen's Park as quickly as possible. Since there was no particular need for democratic processes, a nominating committee (Honsberger, Brown, Cleghorn, Lochead, Williams) had already formulated a list of officers, and this was quickly and unanimously accepted. As figureheads there was an honorary president and vice-president. The former was John Fennell, grand old Victorian gentleman, Berlin's first president of the Board of Trade and still prominent in hardware and insurance. The latter was the equally venerable Robert Smyth, founder of a dry goods company, owner of the Janzen Block in the downtown area, and another former president of the Board of Trade. F.E. Macklin, who also had a dry goods store in the city's centre, was the president, Honsberger was the vice-president, and Harry Brown, teacher of art and mathematics at what is now Kitchener Collegiate Institute (K.C.I.) was secretary/treasurer. But it was the Publicity Committee that constituted the real ginger group, and Williams and Cleghorn placed themselves on this committee, along with Aldermen Master and Hallman. The new organization called itself the British League—though it could equally as well have been called a sub-committee of the Board of Trade.

At the end of a long evening the following resolution was carried unanimously:

> Whereas the members of the British League are of the opinion that the Government of Ontario should again be urged to pass the bill presented to the Private Bills Committee on behalf of the City Council for permission to change the name of the city of Berlin,
>
> Therefore they respectfully request the Council of this city to adopt immediate measures for repeating their former request in such a manner as shall appear to the Council to be most effective.

In the interests of demagoguery it was also decided that City Council should be told to organize a public meeting at which public feeling could be whipped up about the insulting treatment meted out by the Private Bills Committee, and perhaps even more ominously, there was enthusiastic support for the idea of circulating petitions "emphatically protesting" the subversive behaviour of all those citizens who had caused the defeat of Bill 44. That this was, in effect, an attempt to stifle democratic debate by means of indirect threats was of no consequence.

From this point on the British League moved very fast indeed. They immediately demanded that a special session of City Council be called for the following night, Tuesday, April 12. Its purpose was to discuss the motion brought by Cleghorn and Hallman from the British League, and also to get official Council approval for a public meeting at the Star Theatre three days later. The debate "waxed rather hot in spots," and it was only through frequent recourse to gavel-thumping that Hett managed to keep pandemonium at bay. Once again it was Alderman Gross who was at the eye of the storm, more quietly supported by Reid, as he mounted a spirited, though sometimes rather muddled, rearguard action. The outcome, of course, was never in doubt, the make-up of the Council being what it was.

Cleghorn, in speaking to his motion in his own inimitable way, set the tone of the meeting. We British have been vilely insulted by a government committee was the burden of his text. "If we had been before the Reichstag in Berlin, Germany, we could not have been treated with more injustice." Patriotic speakers had been choked off and, indeed, might just as well have been "gassed and had liquid fire served to them." Gross inquired whether this was supposed to constitute an official report and went on to make the inflammatory statement that as far as he could see C.H. Mills had been remarkably fair in his attempt to present the Private Bills Committee with both sides of the question. Master brushed aside this "dense" comment with "how in the name of common sense can a man represent two sides of a question fairly," thereby beautifully illustrating the mind-set of the true propagandist. Gross tried many other tacks — that the Council would only make further fools of themselves if they went back to Queen's Park; that if the British League wanted a public meeting then the British League should call it; that there were a lot of things in Berlin that stank worse than the name — but he was consistently and derisively howled down. Inevitably, hearing himself accused of being pro-German, he challenged all and sundry to a duel (though he doesn't appear to have specified a weapon), and Hett had to thump quite hard to restore order.

One question of political theory that, as we have seen, was crucial to this particular issue (and which indeed seems to be of perennial interest) was of course hotly discussed. If a government has been elected to govern, surely it shouldn't have to hold a public referendum every time it wants to pass a law, even if such a law is unpopular with some. So Hahn, Cleghorn, *et al.* continued to argue, to which Gross could only rather weakly reply that it wasn't fair and that the matter was too important. But he was on a hiding to nothing in this forum anyway, though when the vote finally came to be taken he may have derived some satisfaction from noting that one more alderman, Zettel, had joined himself and Reid in opposing the British Leaguers. That still made it 11 to 3 (and one absentee) in favour of the motion to call an official meeting of public indignation at the Star Theatre on Friday night.

According to the *Telegraph* the meeting at the Star on Friday, April 14, was "large and enthusiastic." According to the *News-Record* it was "poorly attended." In such ways does the media tend to reveal its allegiances. Whether packed or not, the British League had advertised the meeting with considerable cunning. This was not, they maintained, anything to do with the name change. This was a matter of community pride. The city's elected representatives had been abused while simply and innocently doing their duty; they had been treated with contempt, with discourtesy, not to mention contumely, and all good citizens of whatever stripe should come to the aid of the party. Not surprisingly, the meeting was totally partisan, and the name change was the focus of all the speeches.

On the platform were the British League aldermen, and they invited Williams, Lochead, and Honsberger to join them. One significant and curious absentee was the man who was supposed to be chairing the meeting. Dr. Hett sent his regrets; he had been called away on a "serious case (laughter)." Almost everyone seems to have spoken. Lochead received a standing ovation, and in the course of his address fingered C.H. Mills as an obstructer of recruiting, accusing him of trying to use his influence to wangle a friend's son out of the army; Hahn, who was now specializing in snapping at Hett's heels, deplored the mayor's absence and asked why he was tolerated in office; and Dr. Honsberger, whose messianic style was very popular, was in fine form:

> I am going to take a vote tonight to see what sentiment there is for changing the name of the city. I will ask the people of England who are nightly looking into the sky for the appearance of Zeppelins, and breathing a prayer for the protection of their innocent babes that these monsters of the air come to slay. Will they vote to retain the name of Berlin from which those zeppelins come? No. I will ask the people of outraged Belgium if they will have the name of Berlin, whence came the hordes that bayoneted their babes, retained. They will answer no.
>
> I will ask the people of France and Russia and Servia who have felt the scourge of Prussian atrocity and barbaric cruelty if they will have the name retained. They answer No. Yes, I will even go to the spirit world and ask the souls that suffered on the *Lusitania*. They too answer No. There is only one answer that can be made and that is we can't afford to stand before the world as a people who have not the nerve to change the name for the sake of the Empire and its sacred cause. In the name of all that's patriotic we should go before the Legislature again and ask them — to change the name Berlin.

But the man of the evening was Sam Williams. Clearly his amour propre had been badly bruised at Queen's Park, and his performance at the Star that night, which lasted for over an hour, demonstrated that scorned men are no slouches when it comes to hell's fury. Not for him the psychic blather of Honsberger or the recruiting heroics of Lochead. He was interested in facts, and in particular the facts of the past weeks, which he proceeded to recount in self-justifying detail. He was also eager to make personalized attacks on those whom he considered had tricked him or opposed his cause. Mills was a liar. Almost all politicians were duplicitous. McBride was disreputable. Alderman Reid was a turncoat. As for Gross, he had about as much constancy as a weathercock and, worse still, "it has been gossiped on the streets that a certain button man of this city offered his son an automobile if he would not enlist. I wont mention any names. I don't need to." He certainly didn't. The Dominion Button Works (David Gross, Jr., prop.) was a prominent landmark on Water Street.

The conclusion to this tirade demonstrates that though Williams was angry, he was also politically astute.

> Is there any Conservative in the audience who will ever again endorse Mills for re-election? (Loud shouts of No, No)
>
> I am a Conservative, but as long as I live the Hearst Government, or the Hanna Government if it changes to that, will never get a vote from me. If they think they can turn down the British element in this city and get away with it, it is up to us to show them that they are mistaken. Conservatives, you have found that there is corruption in your party. You should punish the party and clean out the corruption. Let every Conservative here tonight sign the statement that he will not vote for Mr. Mills or Hearst again.

One cannot think of any threat, coming as it did from dyed-in-the-wool Conservatives, better calculated to make the party sit up and listen, or at least shift uneasily in its seat. A politician, after all, is as jealous of votes as a squirrel is of nuts.

A lengthy resolution was finally put to the meeting. After a series of "Whereases" it concluded:

> Be it resolved that this open and publicly-called meeting of the citizens of Berlin urge the Mayor and Aldermen to lodge with Premier Hearst a vigorous protest against the discourteous treatment accorded them and their supporters by the Private Bills Committee on Tuesday, April 4, 1916, and against the Committee in throwing out the Bill without hearing any arguments either in its support or otherwise, and
>
> Be it further resolved, that the Mayor and Aldermen press upon Premier Hearst the urgent necessity, both from local and national patriotic considerations, of granting immediate relief from what is fast becoming an intolerable situation, and one which is bound to place the citizens of Berlin, through no fault of their own, in an unfair position in the minds of other loyal citizens of Canada.

The resolution carried unanimously, and the meeting broke up to cheers and "God Save The King."

The Council meeting on Monday night, April 17, was the rowdiest yet. The public seats were packed with a British League cheering section that persistently interrupted the main drama, itself full of bitterness, accusations, and vituperation. As the *Telegraph* reported, the meeting "was anything but creditable to the city during this time of stress." That Hett was able to retain control was remarkable, particularly as he himself was the subject of personal abuse in the course of what looked like an attempt to impeach him.

The meeting began with the inevitable Hallman-Cleghorn motion. It was expressly addressed to Premier Hearst and urgently pressed on him the necessity of immediately changing the name of Berlin. Nor was there any further interest in appearing before a parliamentary committee. Now they "respectfully request that you and your cabinet grant them an interview along with a number of our prominent citizens." There was good reason for this urgency and cutting of corners. The current session of the legislature was coming to an end; indeed, some thought it might be as early as Friday.

As expected, Reid and Zettel immediately moved an amendment to the motion to the effect that both the motion itself and everything pertaining to the name change be tabled until the end of the war. It was, of course, defeated, but now a fourth alderman, Huehnergard, had joined Gross, Reid, and Zettel. The gang of three had become a gang of four, and although the British League's majority on Council was still overwhelming, one wonders whether they were made slightly nervous by these small erosions and as a result became even more determined to ram the whole issue through as quickly as possible.

The debate on the original motion followed predictable lines and, predicatably, Gross provided the powder for the majority of the explosions. The only trouble with Gross was that rather than mustering a disciplined and concentrated fire he seemed to be something of a loose cannon. At various points he called Cleghorn "you dirty, old sneak, you," refuted Williams's insinuation at the Star Theatre that he'd bribed his son with a car not to enlist, and accused Williams of being an American citizen (which caused an uproar in the Council chamber), told the aldermen that they'd just make asses of themselves if they went back to Queen's Park again, and taunted them with the accusation that on the previous occasion they'd made themselves a laughing stock by going off and having dinner at a German hotel.

Voices: It's not a German hotel!
Hahn: The proprietor of the Krausman Hotel is a Canadian, and was born near Zurich!
Gross: Well it's known as a German hotel!
Master: We didn't ask whether it was a German hotel or not. We were after a good meal and we got it!

Whether Gross indulged in his more lively sallies pour épater le bourgeois, or whether he was one of those individuals for whom contrariness is a matter of principle, it is impossible to say, but at least he stuck to his loose cannon and fired it openly — as even his enemies grudgingly admitted. That he did not receive the support of those who essentially agreed with his views was the greatest single weakness of the campaign to retain the name. Both at this meeting and at earlier and subsequent ones, the Cleghorns and Hallmans and Rudells were able freely and accurately to hammer away at the point that the opposition never showed its face at Council or public meetings even though invited to do so and that they themselves obviously, therefore, represented the majority, officially and unofficially. True, the opposition had had a small delegation at Queen's Park, but before and since they seemed to have disappeared into the woodwork. Who were all the supporters they claimed to have, and where were they? Were they cowards? Were they secretly ashamed of their cause? The potential for insinuation was endless.

Needless to say, the invitation to the "opposition" to step forward into the public arena was purely factitious. First of all there was the intimidation factor, and here the punishment meted out to Tappert, the gossip around town that Sergeant Major Blood "had got a little list," and the continuing pillaging of the soldiers, were only the tip of the iceberg; there was also the web of social and business activities that could be negatively affected. Secondly, there was the certainty that a riot would have ensued if an equally aggressive crowd of anti-name-change supporters had actually been mustered to attend Council meetings, for example, and this knowledge surely inhibited the use of such a tactic. It was simply not in the nature of men such as W.H. Breithaupt to indulge in alley fights, and they were hence at a tremendous disadvantage. Victory, in any political situation, in the short term at least, goes to the side willing to spill blood.

Thirdly, there was that old, though still familiar, situation in which political correctness seizes the moral high ground, from whence it is able to make even the voice of reason sound suspect, perhaps even immoral. Knowing this, the voice of reason becomes apologetic and hesitant. Yeats, in famous lines from "The Second Coming" written at about the same time about a different political battle, beautifully summarizes the perennial dilemma: "The best lack all conviction, while the worst/Are full of passionate intensity."

As the stormy meeting progressed, the mayor increasingly came under attack. Cleghorn set the ball rolling with the sarcastic comment that he was sorry that Hett had been unable to chair the meeting at the Star Theatre due to a "serious case," but that he hoped that it had now recovered. Hett replied that though, in fact, he had been called to see a patient, he was prepared to state that there was also a political reason why he didn't attend, this being that he did not care to preside at a meeting which he knew would be nothing more than a vitriolic and bombastic attack on the provincial government. Needless to say, his remarks did little to placate the angry aldermen, and a little later Hahn, whose attacks on his mayor have all the appearance of personal animus, pressed him once more to declare himself on the name change. "Are you a man or a mouse?" he angrily asked, but Hett refused to be drawn. Later still Hahn took the offensive once again:

> Hahn: Does His Worship consider it democratic as a Chief Magistrate to refuse to take a stand on an important question of this kind?
> Hett: The question is out of order.
> Hahn: Then I am convinced you are a mouse!

This bold sally merely elicited the mild reminder that the chair should not be insulted in such a manner. It was as frustrating as pummelling smoke, and Hahn snapped back that as far as he was concerned "the appellation of jellyfish made concerning the mayor a year ago was not soft enough." The comparison was apt to the extent that, whenever he was poked, Hett somehow always returned to his accustomed shape. But the jellyfish prodding was not yet over. When the main Cleghorn-Hallman motion had been voted on and passed (by the expected margin of 11-4), the British Leaguers suddenly slipped in another motion, moved by Hallman and seconded by Rudell. "That the Council is of the opinion that the Mayor should declare himself as to whether he is in favour of changing the name or not." This brought a furious protest from Gross and Reid, who argued that it was a purely personal matter, and that Hett was in an untenable position in view of the two equally strong petitions pro and con the name change. That, of course, was the whole point of the badgering, because presumably everyone knew that a good number of those who were pro-Berlin were Hett supporters, so that to force him to publicly renounce the name would have been a significant coup. After a good deal more argument the motion was put and carried—though now it was to be noted that there were six aldermen who didn't vote for it—and it appeared as though Hett had been finally backed into a corner. I can well imagine the silent anticipation in the Council chamber as he rose to declare his position: "My opinion is that it will be in the best interests of the city to say nothing." The jellyfish had struck again, and, according to the *Telegraph,* "the Council and the spectators in the chamber howled with laughter for several minutes," though whether due to the comedy of the moment or out of derision it doesn't say.

The meeting may have broken up on a raucous note, but its serious purpose was not lost sight of. An urgent request had been addressed to Premier Hearst, and nothing underlines urgency better than a telegram. Within minutes of the ending of the meeting (and surely there was some pre-planning in all this) a night cable was on its way to Queen's Park. At this point one might have expected the sluggish reactions of government to come into play, but amazingly a reply was back in Berlin by noon the next day, Tuesday, April 18. Even more amazingly, a meeting was granted with members of the cabinet the very next morning. It is impossible to say what provoked this sudden acquiescence, though one can well imagine a flurry of behind-the-scenes telephone calls and influence-peddling not unconnected with Williams's threat of a Conservative revolt in Waterloo County.

The British League had to move very fast indeed in order to get a delegation, even bigger and weightier than the previous one, to Toronto in less than 24 hours. The haste, however, had produced one advantage. It caught the counter-petitioners unprepared, and as a result they had no representatives at this second meeting. The deputation included Hett and eight of his aldermen, most of the executive of the British League, as well as Captain Walters and Captain Seagram of the 118th Battalion. They were received by an equally impressive array of ministers:

apart from Lucas, there was R.A. Pyne (Acting Premier), W. Hanna (Provincial Secretary), Findlay McDiarmid (Public Works), and G.H. Ferguson (Lands and Forests).

As before, solicitor Sims led off for the Berlin delegation, and as before he insisted that the name had to be changed and, crucially, that it should not be changed by public vote, as this would tear the city apart. Hallman made the usual claim that there was practically no opposition to the proposal, but omitted to explain why, if there was no opposition, a public vote would be so traumatic. As subsequent speakers reiterated the familiar points, it was noted that the cabinet members began to get impatient to get back to the House, which was already in session. Finally, as Captain Walters began to sing the old refrain once again, Lucas wearily suggested that there was really no point in repeating arguments that they'd all heard before, and the discussion turned slightly acerbic.

> Walters: Then you don't think it is any use saying anything more?
> Lucas: No! I can't see the use.
> Walters: Well I do! I came here to represent the 118th battalion. The turn down by your committee has had a bad effect on recruiting. Some of the Germans up there actually insult our troops on the streets!
> Lucas: Well cramming this name down their throats wont make them any more loyal, will it! How about all the other places with German names? Aren't they all entitled to an act if you are?
> Walters: We from Berlin understand what the change will do a little better than you do!

The meeting was at something of an impasse. Hahn tried to persuade the government that if the Council was allowed to change the name then it would be the Council that would be held to account and not the government, but this piece of casuistry didn't seem to get very far. Finally Lucas announced that he had a solution. He would be prepared to put through a bill right away that would allow any municipality to change its name if a majority of its citizens voted to do so. He was also at pains to point out that he, personally, and of course the Conservatives generally, were not in any way opposed to the petitioner's desires, and indeed thought that their city had a rotten name, but that the government really had to be careful that local councils didn't become, how should he put it, "over-zealous in connection with patriotic measures" — thereby disclosing that the provincial government was under no illusion as to the true state of affairs in Berlin. His "solution," of course, was almost exactly what the Private Bills Committee had originally urged, and what the counter-petitioners had requested, two weeks earlier. It was also what the delegation didn't want (and no doubt they also took silent umbrage at the "over-zealous" slur), but it was a take-it-or-leave-it proposition and time was running out. Grudgingly they took it. A bill was immediately prepared and went through the house that night.

Afterwards, in the corridors outside, there was an *ad hoc* meeting of the City Council. It was agreed that a special session of the full Council should be called for Tuesday night, April 25, at which the by-law for changing the name could be given the necessary readings, and a date for the vote be set. The latter should be as soon as possible, say, three weeks. The Lucas solution was a long way from being satisfactory, but surely with enough noise and energy victory would be theirs and the hated name of the "Hun" capital would disappear forever.

EIGHT

The Referendum Battle

As the French and the Germans performed their interminable dance of death at Verdun, the Canadians geared up for their first serious blooding at Mont Sorrel and the Somme, the Americans continued to dither about whether or not to get in on the act, and Sir Roger Casement prepared to set sail for his sad destiny in Ireland, the citizens of Berlin, Ontario, readied themselves for their own small Armageddon on the issue of a name.

Not that it was clear, even at this stage, that the matter would be put to an immediate public vote. True, the British League aldermen had decided amongst themselves while at Queen's Park that the whole thing should be pushed through with as much dispatch as possible, but it was still necessary to get formal ratification for their timetable at the April 25 session of City Council. And as the six days between the corridor pow-wow and the official council meeting passed, it became increasingly clear that aldermanic support for an early vote was turning a little soft.

There was now really only one strategy open to those who opposed the changing of the name, and this was to try to delay the plebiscite to "a later date." The tactic was an appealing one for a number of reasons. For some there was the hope that "that old common arbitrator Time" would dissipate the highly charged emotions that gripped the city, that reason and common sense would reassert themselves, and the motion would be defeated. Maybe people would lose interest and there would be no vote at all. Maybe the war would end. For others, the moderates, there was genuine concern that the current sporadic lawlessness would escalate into something a great deal worse unless a breathing space were introduced. Indeed, full-scale "race riots" had been predicted by both sides. And finally, tying

114

together all these concerns, was the 118th Battalion, the catalyst for all the rioting. Everyone was fully aware that they would be leaving for their summer camp in the not too distant future, so if the vote could be delayed until after this happy event a successful outcome would be much more likely. Needless to say, the British League wanted a quick vote for precisely opposite reasons. For them, time appeared to be an enemy, and as for the departure of the 118th, it was crucial to have the soldiers around, and not just because of the votes they represented, but for their intimidation value.

As the six days passed, the pressure on the aldermen to change their minds or stand firm increased. As we have seen, four aldermen at the meeting of April 17 had already voted for deferral—Gross, Reid, Zettel, and Huehnergard. By Saturday there were rumours that Gallagher had joined them. If three more could be persuaded to "cross the floor" then the name might well be saved. Much to the *Telegraph's* disgust, "leading citizens" (unidentified, as always) were button-holing possible aldermanic converts or asking other influential businessmen to talk them into line. On Saturday the *News-Record* came out in favour of deferral. With its customary flair for euphemism and understatement, it warned that the discussion had so far been academic. If it came to a vote,

> the citizens would then face an actual condition. Suppressed feelings would gain vent and reach a flood. This would not conduce to the welfare of the community. The agitation which would accompany the submission of the matter to the electors at this time might divide the citizens into two hostile camps. This possible breach would not be bridged in a generation.

It was, then, on the issue of the date of the referendum that battle was to be joined.

At the climactic meeting on the evening of Tuesday, April 25, no one was quite sure which way the vote would go, but the British League made sure that their own version of persuasion was very much in evidence. When the aldermen entered the council chamber, they found not the usual crowd of pro-name-change citizens, commercial travellers, and Board of Traders, but Colonel Lochead and a large contingent of the 118th Battalion. Although it is possible that the soldiers had suddenly become keen students of civic government, it is rather more likely that their presence at this meeting evidenced other motives. One can also assume that they were there with the approval of Lochead. Altogether there were "several hundred" spectators, almost all of them in favour of the name change and eager to participate in the discussion with cheers, catcalls, and other partisan interruptions; and once again Hett's achievement in steering the meeting through to a conclusion was something of a miracle, though whether a fair debate was possible in such circumstances is questionable.

The first motion to be put, whether or not there should be a vote on the name change at all, passed fairly easily, as expected, although there were now five aldermen who voted against it—Gross, Gallagher, Huehnergard, Zettel, and Schwartz. On this occasion Reid voted with the Cleghorn faction, but it was known that he was in favour of deferral, which would bring the number to six. If two more aldermen changed their position the name was in a fair way to being retained.

It was left to the two principal antagonists on the Council to lock horns again when the crucial motion of the date for the public referendum came to the floor. Cleghorn moved that it should be held on Friday, May 19. Gross moved an amendment that it should be January 1, 1917. It was "a warm discussion," with both sides pulling out all the stops in their efforts to out-claim each other, and with the spectators keeping up a constant baying of approval and disapproval. As usual, patriotic passion was much in evidence, but now the commercial arguments, always a factor in the debate, were marshalled with more and more vigour. Evidence of lost business, stories of "Made in Berlin" goods being rejected, and exhortations to change the name from companies as far away as England and New Zealand were all read into the record. Yet the citizens of Berlin could see for themselves that, though there may have been isolated examples of Berlinphobia in the marketplace, generally speaking, the dire predictions of local economic collapse were nonsense. War orders were pouring in, factories were working overtime, and there was little unemployment. Nevertheless, the threat of lost business remained one of the key arguments right to the end of the campaign, and as a tactic it was probably quite effective. It may not have been true, but the fear that it *might* be true if the name wasn't changed, that businesses would relocate, that jobs would be lost, that real estate in this home-owning community would take a nose dive, may have swayed some voters.

Rather more effective, and certainly more interesting, was the confident declaration that sentiment in the city was currently strongly *opposed* to changing the name, and that if a vote were to be taken it would be defeated and the city dishonoured and embarrassed from coast to coast. Had this assertion come from Gross alone one might suspect a certain degree of whistling in the dark, but it was also the opinion of Gallagher, who seems to have been something of an independent.

> Last Sunday I asked a man what he thought the result of submitting it would be. He said that it would be beaten 8 to 1. That same man on Monday morning made it his business to enquire of everybody he came in contact with as to his opinion. In one day he did not meet with one man who said he would vote for it.

This informant, said Gallagher, "was eager to have it submitted. 'I hope they submit it just to show you where you get off at' was a remark made by the gentleman referred to." Though the modern pollster might have reservations about the precision of Gallagher's survey techniques, the results do at least serve as a reminder that the deafening noise of the British League and its supporters, which is about all that Berliners had been hearing for weeks, was not by any means representative of majority opinion.

Gross was quick to support Gallagher, though the odds of 3 to 1 that he quoted were slightly more modest. Of course he presented his arguments in his usual bumptious manner, and when this brought a reaction from the troops, he turned round and called them "hoodlums." This exchange almost provoked a riot, but the combined efforts of Hett, Lochead, and the aldermen brought them under control, while Hahn, with amazing cheek considering his own behaviour, piously admonished his fellow alderman to remember where he was and his position. One doubts whether Gross felt chastened.

The rest of the debate followed a well-worn pattern, with various aldermen declaring that there was no need to rehearse the old arguments and then proceeding to do so at some length. Those in favour of delaying the vote were called traitors and pro-German, and the accusations were duly objected to. Cleghorn maintained that changing the name would increase enlistment in the 118th, and fingered the Langs (now popularly assumed to be, with W.H. Breithaupt, the main power behind the anti-name-change lobby) for obstructing recruiting efforts. Gross countered with a characteristic irrelevance by asking why Cleghorn's daughters hadn't volunteered to become nurses. The legal costs of changing the name became an issue of charge and counter-charge, with Gross suggesting that of course the lawyers were in favour of it because they'd be making a lot of money.

Finally exhaustion set in and with Gallagher, for some reason, in the chair, the vote was taken. In favour of May 19 were Master, Ferguson, Hahn, Hallman, Cleghorn, Hessenauer, Dunke, Rudell, and Schnarr. Opposed were Gross, Huehnergard, Zettel, Schwartz, Reid, and Hett. Nine to six. In exactly 24 days, the citizens of Berlin would be presented with a ballot containing the simple question: "Are you in favour of changing the name of this city?"

At the end of the proceedings the mayor desperately pleaded for sanity in the coming campaign, and asked the members of Council for their co-operation in bringing this about. There was almost no hope that his wishes would be met. Not only was the issue an emotional one, but all the evidence suggested that the electorate was split right down the middle. Indeed, if Gross and Gallagher may be believed, there may even have been a slight majority in favour of retaining the name. If this were the case then it only redoubled the resolution of the British League. And they had several formidable weapons in their armoury. First of all they were convinced that they bore before them the righteous banner of patriotism. Secondly, they had no inhibitions about conducting a strident and very public campaign, and they were prepared to go to any extreme, questionable or not, to win. Thirdly, and most importantly, they had an efficient organization which understood the importance of house-to-house surveys, getting out the vote, and so on. And of course they had the 118th Battalion.

Evidence that the British League was carefully planning ahead came, indeed, in a cunning move at the end of this very meeting. A committee was created to draft a list of poll clerks and deputy returning officers for election day. It consisted of Hahn, Hallman, Cleghorn, Master, Rudell, and Gallagher, who thus came to control, to some extent, voting procedures and regulations. Gross seems to have smelt something of a rat and argued for a different committee. He was unsuccessful.

That the 118th Battalion would be a potent force was attested to by their presence at the meeting. Word was now coming through from militia headquarters that they would be moving to London in four weeks. In fact, three days after the vote. The timing was not lost on the citizens of Berlin. Like two equal plots in a well-made play, the intertwined histories of the city and its battalion were destined to reach a messy denouement together.

The *Telegraph*, in an editorial, was delighted to learn that the lads would be around for the campaign, not only because of the votes they represented, but also because they would be able to influence the campaign, though it didn't define "influence." Police Constable Blevins, however, had a pretty good idea what it entailed and would probably have been just as happy to wave them goodbye a lot earlier. On Monday night, April 24, he had gone to the barracks to have a chat with Private Meinzinger, a man well known for his pugilistic abilities, about a small matter of assault. Meinzinger had apparently been doing some enthusiastic recruiting, probably in the bar of the Brunswick Hotel, and in particular had tried to persuade a man called Henry Halling to enlist. Halling had a Medically Unfit card, but Meinzinger said it was a fake, tore it up and then worked over the unfortunate Halling. It was this little affray that Constable Blevins came to talk about, but Meinzinger hardly let him get started. A right-hander broke one side of his jaw and a left-hander broke the other, and Blevins was carted off to hospital. This assault was too much even for the Berlin military authorities, and Meinzinger got 18 months in the Guelph Prison Farm and was drummed out of the army. If nothing else, the incident graphically explains the reluctance of the local constabulary to take on the soldiers.

The Recruiting Committee had, meanwhile, decided to make one final effort to bring the battalion up to strength. In letters to the press, Lochead had once again warned that "there is a grave probability that the 118th O.S. Battalion will lose its identity as a military unit if it is not recruited to practically full strength before we leave Berlin for London." With only three or four weeks left, it was a little late for conjuring rabbits from hats, let alone blood from stones, but everything had to be tried. Rumours of a new initiative had been circulating since the end of the 700 Men In Three Weeks campaign, and it was claimed that it would be both unique in character and certain of success. The secret weapon turned out to be women. The "fair sex" was to be thrown into the breech (though not into breeches, which would have to wait for later wars) in an all-out venture to be officially called The Ladies' Ten Day Campaign, to be headed up, appropriately, by Mrs. Lochead. At the organizational meeting at the barracks on Wednesday, April 19, 200 ladies turned up to be briefed on means and methods. Basically it was to be a fun competition, and to this end the ladies were divided up into 18 teams of 10, and 18 captains were elected for each team. Each team was expected to "capture" as many men as possible, and the winning team was to get $250, the second team $150, and the third team $100, though the women quickly agreed to give the prize money to some patriotic fund.

The campaign kicked off with another "monster parade" on a beautiful Saturday evening, April 29. The standard estimate of 10,000 people lined beflagged and bebuntinged King Street, or leaned out of windows and balconies from city hall down to the Kaufman factory, awaiting the arrival of the female warriors. Meanwhile, outside the barracks on Queen Street South the women, decked out in khaki suits, were being juggled into columns of four by the officers of the 118th, and when all was ready Colonel Lochead barked them into motion. Preceded by the band of the 118th and "Czar" (and perhaps the collie), they came down Queen Street and on to King, waving their banners bearing potent slogans such as "If You Wont We Will" and "We Would Go If We Could" and "Protect Your Wives And Mothers." At the train tracks they wheeled about and marched back up King, returning to the barracks, where they were dismissed to begin their recruiting efforts.

No doubt in the days that followed the ladies did their best to inveigle eligible young men into uniform, but it was all a bit like casting colourful lures into an overfished pond. The press carried one or two stories about their efforts. There was the lady, for example, who marched into a haberdasher's, was waited on by a young man, ordered half a yard of yellow ribbon and then told him to keep it. Another male clerk, who was reported to have gotten fresh with one of the fair recruiters, was threatened with swift and all too familiar retribution. "That this young 'Gentleman' will pay dearly for his indiscretion is certain," warned the *News-Record*, "for the soldiers have him on their list and woe betide Mr. 'Freshy' when they get their hands on him. Let this be a warning to Berlin's young men." The sex of the recruiters had changed; the attitude was depressingly familiar. But to expect the women to enlist the required 450 men was a forlorn hope, and the papers soon ceased to follow their campaign. In the end they were credited with getting some 40 more men into uniform.

On Tuesday, May 2, a week after the City Council had set May 19 as the date for the public referendum, the British League held a meeting at city hall to set up a special organization, the By-Law Committee, to make sure that the vote went their way. As a gathering of the converted it was as much pep rally as planning session, but then no one was under any illusion that the campaign was going to be a cakewalk. Indeed, there was even a touch of pessimism here and there about the outcome of the vote, and grave warnings were issued about the amount of proselytizing that would have to be done. At least one speaker corroborated the findings of the opposition's street polls; in informal chats he had discovered that five out of eight would vote against a new name.

Some time was spent on the relative vote-catching merits of patriotic as opposed to commercial arguments. Lip service was paid to the precedence of the former because it was the nominal ideal, but as most businessmen tend to be more comfortable with balance sheets than ideals, they were much happier discussing the latter. It was W.C. Burns, the president of Monarch Oil, who summarized what the main thrust of the campaign would have to be when he insisted that "the bread and butter side would be the strongest argument among the electors and would have to be used." (Whether the campaign concerns changing names or sovereignty, the Hit Them In Their Wallets tactic is always the most effective one.)

To this point the meeting had been cautious, if not sombre. Clearly a spot of stiffening the sinews and summoning up the blood was required, and on this occasion the metaphor was made flesh when the redoubtable Sergeant Major himself stepped forward to put patriotic fervour back on the agenda. He boldly reminded the assembled business folk that the poor were probably less worried about losing money than they were and then lashed into any German person or institution that was antagonistic to British sentiment. They were to be "wiped out" and "smashed." "We're going to make Berlin and North Waterloo Canadian or make them get out. Get in line and be British! Get in khaki! Remember there will never be a chance to be of German sentiment after the war! Therefore change the name!" George DeBus rather meekly wondered whether the word "Prussian" or "Hun" might be substituted for German so as not to hurt people's feelings. After all, his own mother was German. But Blood brushed this aside. Obviously he was only referring to pro-German Germans, not anti-German Germans. As for the suggestion that the vote could be lost, well this was simply not going to happen. "You have nothing to fear," he vowed, and then added somewhat enigmatically, "you have the support of 300,000 Canadian soldiers, and millions of others in the Empire who are out to declare war on pro-Germans."

This little touch of Granville in the night was received with tremendous applause, and the meeting then turned to ways and means. J.A. Hallman was elected chairman, and four committees were formed, each one consisting of six or seven prominent men. Each committee was assigned to one of the five city wards. L.J. Breithaupt and A.R. Kaufman, who now seem to have joined the name-changers, were in the Centre Ward committee along with Cleghorn, DeBus, Sims, and Eby. Each committee was charged with the job of conducting a house-by-house canvass of every street in their ward so that every friendly voter would be identified — and every opponent. Ward meetings were to be arranged and street corner discussions encouraged. Larger meetings were to be held in the downtown theatres, and factory owners were encouraged to get their employees together for short lectures on the consequences of not changing the name. Slogans were suggested, the feasibility of hiring conveyances to get supporters to the polls was discussed, and assurances that citizens would be able to choose the new name in a subsequent vote were made. The meeting broke up in a spirit of optimism. There was certainly a lot to be accomplished, but at least an organization was in place and a plan of action approved. Of anything similar from the opposition there was no sign at all. There were 17 days left to polling day.

Three days later, as if to give point to Blood's promise that the army was going to "declare war on pro-Germans," the Acadian Club rooms in Waterloo were wrecked by a mob of soldiers from the 118th. Essentially this was a rerun of the Concordia Club episode, though the Acadian Club does not seem to have been in any way a hotbed of pro-Germanism. Indeed, 28 of its 60 to 80 members had already enlisted, though this didn't save its tables, chairs, pictures, lamps, curtains, chandeliers, and a piano from destruction. It is also unknown whether Blood himself had anything to do with the demolition. N.A. Zick, the club president, stated in his report that "the leader of the party who raided the Club was a member who had not paid his dues for a considerable period," but such details were irrelevant in the climate of the times. The essential message conveyed to all and sundry was that the 118th was very much alive and well (and uncontrollable) and no one could expect to escape the long arm of its lawlessness. The resolution of the affair is also instructive. The club asked the battalion for damages of $529.75. After an inquiry it was agreed that the battalion was responsible but shouldn't have to pay because "further ill-feeling might be engendered." Costs were reassessed at $355.65, and the army asked to foot the bill. Sam Hughes agreed and sent the bill to the Privy Council, who sent it to the Department of Justice, which "decided that the claim cannot be entertained. We have a number of similar claims, one at Calgary, another at Winnipeg, and perhaps others, and the view of the Minister of Justice is that there is no legal responsibility on the part of the Crown." So the Acadian Club got nothing, though there might have been some consolation in the thought that there were other places in Canada where soldiers were undisciplined.

In the next week or two the tension in Berlin continued to increase. There were the usual recruiting meetings at which "the young men of the city were as scarce as pork butcher shops in Palestine," the ladies continued to trawl for young men who might be enticed into uniform, and the people continued to supply the press with reasons why the name should or should not be changed — though some of these probably did little to promote the cause they espoused. There was, for example, the gentleman who was opposed to changing the name because "all humanity is a seething mass of corruption. . . . and Sodom and Gommarah [*sic*] would not have escaped destruction had other names been substituted," so what was the point. Then there was a peculiar squabble between "New Zealander" and "Outsider." The former began by writing a turgid letter supporting the name change. "Outsider" took offence at "the inane nature of the diatribe" and, perhaps illogically, suggested that outsiders should mind their own business. Whereupon "New Zealander" replied with what one takes to be kiwi invective, suggesting that if "Outsider" was "as small in stature as he is in principles he could kiss his boots without bending his knees and that when he dies a peanut shell will serve to coffin his body." Perhaps the citizens of Berlin, like Canadians before and since, were secretly delighted that foreigners were taking such a keen interest in their affairs. This impulse may also have been behind the *Telegraph's* story that several prominent English newspapers were writing about Berlin and urging it to change its name. The "prominent" newspapers were the *Exeter Flying Post*, the *Surbiton Times*, the *Andover Advertiser*, and the *Fenwick Gazette*.

The passions of the moment also prompted some Berliners to burst into verse as a heightened means of making their point. The *News-Record* printed some of these, such as "The Two Berlins" which ran, or rather galloped,

Berlin, in Prussia, is on the river Spree,
A very "kultured" city people say,
With palaces and gardens and statues by the score,
While countless soldiers "goose-step" every day.

And so on. This was followed by "The Name."

There's a city in Ontario
And it's known far and near
And the citizens are proud of it
And its name they hold most dear.
But now a cloud hangs over it
And on its name a stain.
They tell us we must bury it
With bitter tears and shame.

More noteworthy (for its ambition rather than its execution) was the parody, "The Britisher's Soliloquay" (*sic*).

To change or not to change our name,
That is the question.
Whether 'tis more British to suffer
Commercial loss after the war,
Or now to take a plebiscite in a sea of trouble,
And by a vote end it.
To kill, to crush, to sleep, and
By a change to say we end luke-warm sentiment,
And the thousand slackers this city is heir to.
'Tis a consummation devoutly to be wished.
To kill! To crush! To sleep! Perchance to dream!
Ay, there's the rub;
For even with another name what slurs may come
When we have shuffled off "Berlin"
Must give us pause.
There's the unfilled battalion that makes
Calamity of our sudden spurt of loyalty.
For we must bear the whips and scorns of time,
The Dominion's contumely for lip loyalty
That gave not men when Britain called.
The pangs and arrows will reach our core
For a name is but a tinsel shield
Against just accusations rightly fired.
We ourselves might, with a full battalion,
Even now under our present name, prevent
Much future grunting and swearing
Through a weary life.
But lo! it is that fearful dread
Of something after war

The dwindling trade when travellers return,
With empty order books and ill,
That makes us haste to change our name;
And in our haste forget to fill our own battalion
Although she cries aloud for men.
Thus future trade makes patriots of us all,
And thus a belated plebiscite is sicklied o'er
With the pale cast of loyalty,
And enterprises of great pith and moment,
With this regard, their currents turn awry,
And cry with one accord: "Let us change our name."

One can imagine the anguished spinning in a certain Stratford grave.

On Thursday, May 11, eight days before voting day, those opposed to the name change (or the Stand Patters, as the *Guelph Mercury* dubbed them) dropped their one and only bombshell into the campaign, when an injunction to prevent the vote taking place was served on the City Council. The legal grounds for the injunction were that the city had passed its by-law authorizing the vote before the Lieutenant-Governor had given assent to the special act allowing it to do so. The injunction was to be heard on May 18, the day before the vote. Whether the move was supposed to have anything more than the nuisance value of a delaying tactic is hard to say. Sims, the city's lawyer, doubted whether the injunction would be successful and advised Council to oppose it, but nevertheless it meant that a small cloud of uncertainty hovered over the proceedings of the next few days.

The injunction was brought by William Kingsley, the 36-year-old Berlin factory worker who had earlier attacked Cleghorn in the press, and was delivered to the Berlin Council by McBride. It was a questionable tactical move. No one, of course, believed that Kingsley himself had instigated the application, and so once again the British League could, probably with some justification, upbraid their shadowy opponents for not having the courage to come out into the open and do their own dirty work. Furthermore, they could derisively laugh at them for, first of all fighting for a public referendum on the name change, and then, having got their way, turning around and trying to quash it. But whether Kingsley was a front man or not, his role in the controversy serves as a reminder, if any is needed, that politics and class were as much a feature of the name-change debate as racial origins. When asked why he wasn't in uniform, Kingsley swiftly replied that he was a socialist—thereby endorsing and extending the recent Canadian Labour Congress motion in Vancouver decrying conscription. In the end Kingsley dropped the injunction the day before it was to be heard.

As was to be expected, the last few days of the campaign were charged with bitterness, though the details of the battle have to be discerned through the obscuring smoke of opposing broadsides. As well, the two newspapers seem to have been reluctant to report some of the more lurid stories, perhaps in an attempt to dampen passions (neither, for example, reported the Acadian Club affair) so it is sometimes necessary to reconstruct events from hints and vague allusions.

Immediately after the Blevins-Meinzinger incident, Hett (who had set the constable's broken jaw) met with O'Neill, the Chief of Berlin's small police detachment, to discuss the whole situation of law and order in the city. Both were well aware that the officers of the 118th had little control over their men and that the police were incapable of handling the expected riots, and both concluded that the only answer was to try to get a detachment of military police stationed in the city until the troops had left for London. That such a move was long overdue must have been obvious to everyone, but when Hett discussed the idea with the City Council it was blocked. The reason was obvious. The British League aldermen considered the soldiers to be their storm troopers, and they didn't want their activities curtailed in any way.

As the days leading up to the election passed, Hett received more and more appeals for help from those whose persons, homes or businesses had been threatened and who were fearful of some sort of orgy of destruction by the soldiers—particularly if the vote was lost. Eventually, Hett took the initiative and, without telling his aldermen what he was doing, requested help from Ottawa, repeating his belief that some sort of military protection was urgently required. On Saturday, May 13, General Hodgins came down from Ottawa and joined Colonel Shannon, O.C. 1st Division, London, at the Walper House in an informal investigation. They met "privately" with Hett and, according to the *Toronto Daily Star,* some "dozen other prominent gentlemen." Amongst their number were W.H. Breithaupt, August Lang, Gross, W.V. Uttley of the *News-Record,* C.H. Mills, and Scully. In other words, more or less the same men who were involved in the earlier delegation to Queen's Park and who represented the core of the opposition to the name change. They complained about harassing phone calls, defaced property, being kept awake at night by one means or another, and various unspecified "midnight escapades of a few men of the 118th Battalion." Hodgins and Shannon listened, harrumphed a bit, went up the street to the barracks where they listened to Lochead and his officers, harrumphed some more, ordered the men to be called on parade, gave them a brief lecture about responsible civic behaviour, told them they were splendid men all, and left town.

This lack of any sort of resolution to their problem was the worst possible outcome for the Stand Patters. Not only did they fail to get the 118th Battalion moved out of the city, which, if it was their primary intention, was a forlorn hope anyway for reasons of logistics, if not bureaucratic inertia, but they also aroused the Furies which were not anyway sleeping very peacefully in the breasts of the British League. Lochead was livid. Not only had his authority been circumvented, but he had also suffered the indignity of being "reported to the headmaster." And on top of that, the humiliating story had been reported in the *Toronto Daily Star*. On Monday, May 15, all the city's papers, including the *Berliner Journal*, carried the following disclaimer from Lochead:

To The Public Of Berlin.
Regarding the reports apparently more or less generally circulated throughout the city, that the Officers, N.C.O.'s and men of the 118th Battalion mean to take an active part in the election slated for Friday, I beg to state that I myself and every other Officer of the Battalion, pledge ourselves that nothing of the kind was ever suggested or contemplated, and that no soldier will take any part in said election beyond the polling of his vote. Approximately 100 of the officers and men have votes, and these will be given only sufficient leave to proceed to the polls to register their votes; otherwise the Battalion will carry on as usual.

Again, in reference to the reports that the soldiers mean to carry on a campaign of property destruction and of general riot before being moved from the city, I beg to state that I, as Officer commanding, pledge my word of honour that nothing of this character will ever take place, or was ever contemplated so far as I can learn. In this connection I am glad to add that every Officer, N.C.O. and man has pledged himself that he will not misconduct himself in any manner during the remainder of his stay in Berlin. Let me assure the public that they may rest perfectly easy in this regard.

W.M. Lochead
Lieut. Col. O.C. 118th O.S. Battalion, C.E.F.

Whether the public, knowing Lochead's track record, was comforted by this letter is open to doubt. The last phrase of the first paragraph, for example, was hardly likely to set their minds at rest.

When the City Council discovered what had happened they were equally furious, and at the Council meeting held on the same Monday as the letters appeared, and attended by Lochead and his men, the wretched Hett was put through the proverbial wringer. As one might have expected, it was Hahn, positively quivering with delicious indignation, who "precipitated the storm which had been pending since the cat was let out of the bag on Saturday." He was followed by Master, who read out the *Toronto Daily Star* article, and particularly referred to the "prominent men" who had met with Hodgins and Shannon. "It must be that the City Council is not very prominent, as I know of only one of its members that was invited to be present."

Hett: I am surprised at the article in *The Star*, and I assure you that I knew positively nothing about it until you read it just now. In regard to the meeting with the officers from Ottawa and London, I wish to state that the gentlemen were here because numerous complaints have been sent to Ottawa regarding local conditions. You may not know the large number of complaints which reached me coming from people who were frightened lest some depredation might be committed by the soldiers. Many asked me for protection, especially for their property, which they claimed was threatened. Many rumours came in also of what was going to happen when the 118th Battalion left for camp, and of what would take place if the name of the city was not changed on Friday at the polls. The police were powerless and many people were awfully frightened.

Hahn: I guess no one was more "awfully" frightened than yourself.

Hett: (Ignoring Ald. Hahn) Living under such conditions should there not have been an investigation? I sent a communication to Ottawa.

Hahn: (Interrupting) Just one?

Hett: More than one. We don't want riots. I have a great regard for the 118th Battalion and all the men in it. But some have done indiscreet things. In view of this I feel I was perfectly justified in calling for an investigation for the sake of peace and harmony. In regard to the men at the meeting, I was given only ten minutes to get a few men together.

Cleghorn: Will you name the men who were at the conference?

Hett: I do not think I should.

Hahn: You did not think you should take the City Council into your confidence in this matter?

Hett: Some time ago at the meeting of the Police Commission I brought up the matter of having military police to prevent possible trouble. I failed. Disturbances occurred. I brought the matter before the Council at a Finance Meeting. The Finance Committee didn't support me, although a few of the members did. In view of everything I was perfectly justified in not asking the Council.

Master: The letter you sent to Ottawa was founded on rumours. You knew that the City Council would not back up mere rumours.

Rudell: This is a disgrace, coming as it does from the Mayor. It seems too bad that the Mayor must run away and take with him prominent men, who do not want their name exposed, to investigate military conditions in this city. I say it is a contemptible attempt to discredit the 118th Battalion. Common courtesy has not been extended to the Battalion in this matter. The City Council has been ignored.

Hahn: You had with you men opposed to the change of the name of the city. You tried to make out that the Battalion here was going to interfere with the polling of the vote at Friday's election. You have tried to make out that the Battalion was going to intimidate the citizens. You tried to get the Battalion away before they could have a chance to vote. I believe that this Council should vote a lack of confidence in the Mayor.

Master: This whole thing has been done to prejudice the election on Friday. This is the most damnable thing that has ever happened.

Hett: I had no other motive but the harmony and peace of the community.

Hahn: Why did you wait until now? Why did you wait until it was almost time to vote on the by-law before starting this thing? Why did you refer to the interference with the voting that you believed the Battalion would commit. Did you really believe the soldiers would be allowed to block the election?

Cleghorn: Did you not have the officers brought here to have the Battalion removed before the vote was taken?

Hett: (After a number of evasive answers) I did, if we could
           not have order at the election.
Cleghorn: You would not let the soldiers who were going to
           fight for you have a vote?
Hahn: You wanted to get the Battalion out so that the 100
           men in the Battalion who have votes could not have
           polled their votes.

And so the badgering went on until everyone got tired of the
exercise, and a vote of no confidence in the mayor was proposed
and passed, the usual nine aldermen voting in favour, and the
other six abstaining.

The second piece of business at this meeting was far less
dramatic but far more significant. Several days earlier, Hett had
made a public statement to the effect that everyone on the previous voters' list would be eligible to take part in the name-
change referendum. The British League, however, realized that
voter eligibility might hold the key to the winning of the referendum, and Cleghorn, who was nothing if not shrewd, moved that
the city clerk, after consultation with the city solicitor, should
publish an official notice as to who was *legally* entitled to vote.
The notice appeared in the papers the following day, Tuesday,
May 16, just three days before the vote.

The persons entitled to vote upon the question to be submitted
to the electors on the 19th instant are those whose names are
entered on the last revised Voters' List as entitled to vote at
Municipal Elections, and each such voter must be (a) a male, a
widow or an unmarried woman; (b) of the full age of 21 years;
(c) *a British subject by birth or naturalization,* [my italics] and
(d) not disqualified under The Municipal Act or otherwise disqualified from voting. In case of a tenant he shall not be entitled
to vote unless he is a resident of the Municipality at the date of
voting and has resided therein for one month next before such
date and in case of an income voter and of a farmer's son, he is
a resident at the date of voting.
Dated 16th May, 1916
A.H. Millar, City Clerk.

More than meetings, rallies, slogans, editorials, poems, and military intimidation whether real or imaginary, it was this notice
that signalled defeat for those who wished to retain the name of
Berlin.

NINE

The Vote

In private as well as in public one topic must have dominated
the thoughts of Berliners during the last week of the campaign.
In drawing rooms and on street corners, in offices and shops, on
sidewalks, in parks and schools, and barrooms, pool halls, and
clubs, "The Vote" must surely have been debated with the usual
mixture of passion and reason. So far as anyone could tell, the
contestants appeared to be neck and neck as they approached
the wire, though in terms of public pronouncements the British
Leaguers held the initiative by a wide margin. Scare tactics were
now clearly the focus of their campaign, as citizens were warned
that if the name was not changed businesses would relocate,
property prices would fall, jobs would be lost, taxes would rise,
and weeds would soon be growing in the streets. The many published reports of meetings and advertisements and open letters
of CEOs to their workers all carried dire predictions of this
nature. "If you own property and have to pay increased taxes
which is inevitable," said the Retail Merchants, "you are not
likely to take a chance on retaining the name which may cause
property values and wages to go down," while a letter "From
Employer To Employee" warned that loss of sales due to the
name

> means loss to everybody, you and me and our families. It means
> loss to the city as a whole, and loss to every activity within its
> gates. The only thing which will flourish is taxes, and fewer
> people will have to raise them. We will invite disaster by refus-
> ing to change the name.

Even the public school children were roped into the act
when they were reported, two days before the vote, to have
come out overwhelmingly in favour of changing the name (at
Suddaby Public School it was 453 to 0), though the fact that the

motion put to them was "Are you in favour of changing the city's name for patriotic reasons?" and the vote was a standing one may account for this result. This dubious lesson in the democratic process did not, however, prevent the *Telegraph* from sermonizing on the text, "and a little child shall lead them." The day before the vote, this paper's headline cried "KING GEORGE IS WAITING FOR BERLIN'S ANSWER." Beneath it a picture of the waiting monarch stares out at the reader — though his expression appears to be not so much nervous expectation as royal catatonic.

There were, of course, one or two visible signs of opposition to this bulk of propaganda. For example, there was J.F. McKay, the former chairman of the Board of Health, a fierce sage whose voluminous white moustaches gave him the appearance of a dragon breathing smoke from its nostrils. He was also an indomitable opponent of the name change and an obsessive writer of long, tortured letters to the press, in one of which he argued that the word "berlin" was totally inoffensive for it was of Slavic origin and meant "flaxseed," and that as the Russians were Slavs and our allies there was no need to change it. One doubts that he gained many converts. There were also two full-page advertisements in the *News-Record* urging people to vote "No" in the referendum, dismissing the doomsday scenarios of the name-changers, and decrying their insulting and violent tactics. It was signed "The Committee" — another example of anonymity that, of course, drew further insults from their opponents. W.H. Breithaupt, however, who was undoubtedly one of "The Committee," was not afraid of going public. For example, he went personally to the barracks to protest to Lochead about the behaviour of the soldiers in the last two weeks of the campaign, behaviour of which he was provably one of the victims. The day before the vote he wrote a signed letter to the *Toronto Daily Star* in which he reaffirmed the earlier stories of intimidation and expressed the essence of what he was fighting for. "I know directly that many prominent Canadians throughout the country approve the attitude of those who have some feeling of reverence for long established things of good repute, some background of history, and who want to retain an honest name."

Election day, Friday, May 19, was a mixture of sunshine and cloud, and a chilly wind was blowing. As the day wore on, reports came in from the 23 polling stations of steady activity. Voters were turning up in greater numbers than had ever before been recorded for a municipal election — though some had hoped that there might be even more — and cars from both sides were ferrying supporters backwards and forwards. It was also noted that there were large numbers of scrutineers at the entrances to the polling stations. Most of these appeared to be British League supporters, and frequent arguments were observed and much anger when long-term residents were turned away. Even so, when the polls closed at six o'clock it was still anybody's guess as to who had won.

The count began immediately at city hall, and shortly before 7:00 o'clock Millar, the city clerk, announced the first result. It was from the Mansion Street poll in the East Ward, a British League stronghold; 63 for, 41 against. Probably poll 11, just down the hall in the Police Court, came in next; 111 for, 85 against. The roars of approval from the assembled crowd, all of them British League supporters — to have cheered for the opposition in this forum would have been about as judicious as cheering for turkeys at Christmas — was deafening. But when the five polls from the predominantly German North Ward came in, the noise of celebration died down. They came out against the name change by a total of 403 to 235. Once again the two sides were level-pegging, though the Stand Patters would have noted with considerable anxiety that the votes in their favour from the North Ward were not nearly as overwhelming as they had hoped.

The issue was in doubt until the last two polls, which were tabulated around 7:30 p.m. The final score was 1,569 in favour of changing the name, and 1,488 against. The referendum was approved by 81 votes. Out of a voting population of some 5,000, 3,057 citizens cast ballots, for a turnout of just over 60 percent.

The victory parade was the noisiest that the city had ever witnessed. Headed by the band of the 108th Regiment, a line of cars, each one packed with civilians and soldiers, with more perched on bumpers and footboards or dancing and gyrating alongside, set slowly off down King Street. Whether anyone actually heard the military music is doubtful as it had to compete with the tremendous cacophony of non-stop cheering and singing, the constant blaring of car horns, and the frequent explosions of firecrackers and rockets that were let off indiscriminately, causing several injuries. The procession proceeded down to Francis Street and then made a right turn up to Weber. Here it made another right turn and came down to Queen where it made a short jog northwards in order to deliver a little jingoistic taunt in front of Lang's house at 76 Queen North, which still stands today, just

opposite the library. What happened here was described, rather
defensively, by Lochead to Major-General Hodgins.

> The Langs were bitterly opposed to the changing of the name
> and took a very active part throughout the day. Naturally the
> parade stopped at the Lang homestead to give them cheers. Mr.
> August Lang, who had altercations with different civilians
> throughout the day, deliberately walked from the house to the
> street, having in his hand a large walking stick. His manner was
> most defiant and very apparently was courting trouble. On
> reaching the street pavement he immediately got in an argu-
> ment with some civilians which ended in his slashing at one of
> these civilians with his stick. The blow missed the civilian and
> fell on a soldier. Mr. Lang then struck out violently with the
> stick until finally the stick was taken from him and he was
> escorted back to the house by one of the soldiers. I have assur-
> ances from the most reliable men in Berlin that Mr. Lang him-
> self was altogether to blame for the little mix-up and that prima-
> rily it was an affair which concerned civilians and that any part
> which the few soldiers did play was most commendable to
> them. Several of our best citizens assured me that it was deliber-
> ately planned by Mr. Lang so that he would be able to report to
> the authorities bad conduct on the part of the soldiers. Whether
> this is true or not I cannot say but I can absolutely assure you
> that no blame can possibly be attached to the soldiers.

Lochead's pathetic eagerness to whitewash his men may be put
beside the joking report in the *Guelph Mercury* that described
the same scene.

> The procesh, probably more by design than accident, paraded
> past the home of one of the big men of the burg, and the
> charivari of auto snorts was turned on with all the stops pulled
> out and a full head of steam on. A brother of the serenaded
> Stand Patter waltzed out on the sidewalk. It was quite natural
> there should be some conversation. The conversation drifted
> into words that smoked, and there was pepper in the air. It is
> alleged that the wrathy Stand Patter swatted a couple of the vic-
> torious Name Changers over the frontispiece with his walking
> stick. Of course the Name Changers had won one fight and they
> were keen for another. Marquis of Queensbury rules governed,
> and a couple of black eyes worn by one of the leading citizens of
> Berlin tell the story better than the French official communiqué
> could ever hope to do.

Back at city hall the inevitable speechifying was remarkable for
its total absence of magnanimity. This was an enemy that

deserved to have its face ground into the dirt. Sam Williams, who seems to have been credited with spearheading the victory, declared Hett to be "the poorest mayor who ever held office in this city" and called for his resignation (prolonged applause and cheering).

> I say that this man Hett is not worthy or fit to hold office as Mayor of this new city. Where is the Mayor tonight that he is not taking part in this celebration (shouts from crowd). "He has a serious case" (derisive laughter). The work of the opposition in this campaign has shown us that there are dirty Huns in this city who are the same kind as the Prussians we detest.

He then proceeded once again to work out his spleen on the men who had thwarted him before the Public Bills Committee, especially Sir Adam Beck, who "betrayed your interests," C.H. Mills, who "is as good as buried," and Ed Scully, who "will be buried with him." There was more baying for blood from the likes of Hahn, Rudell, and Hallman, the last of whom had just fired off a telegram setting the mind of his monarch at rest as to the outcome of the vote. "The loyal citizens of Berlin, Canada," he wired, "rejoice to inform Your Majesty that they have cast off forever the name of the Prussian capital." One would like to think that George V heaved a sigh of relief. The celebration concluded with the national anthem, though the car horns and fireworks continued long into the night. Half the citizens, of course, or probably rather more than half, remained sadly at home through it all.

It is worthwhile to try to come to an accurate assessment of the fairness of the campaign to change the name of Berlin. In a subsequent petition to the provincial government requesting that the vote be overturned, it was claimed that the promoters of the by-law had employed dishonest, illegal, and intimidating tactics. As we have seen, their opponents vehemently denied this during the campaign and continued to do so after it. Of two witnesses to these events still living in Kitchener, one is quoted as saying, "It wasn't a fair vote," but the other believes that it was. Perhaps it's a difference of perception, or rather a matter of distinguishing where the legitimate rough and tumble of politics ends and more sinister actions that undermine the democratic process begin.

That intimidation was a feature of the campaign there can be no doubt—whether or not there were specific, provable instances during the campaign itself. The soldiers had already shown what they were capable of at the Concordia and Acadian Clubs, in the beating administered to Tappert, and in the numerous fights they provoked while recruiting. And then there was Blood's little black book. It is therefore possible to state that, whether true or not, the mere rumour that the soldiers were going to take an active part in the voting was understandably believed. As a result many people were afraid, and it is reasonable to assume that some of them stayed away from the polls in order to avoid trouble.

There were many charges that the soldiers actually interfered with the democratic process, but these are more difficult to prove. The British League, of course, simply said that all the defacing of property and anonymous threats, and so on, which were certainly a feature of the campaign, were the work of civilians. One of the charges, however, is demonstrably true. In his meeting with Hodgins and Shannon, W.H. Breithaupt, amongst other complaints, said that his phone had been cut. Lochead and his chums riposted as usual that this was all an invention aimed at discrediting the soldiers, but on May 13, six days before the vote, Breithaupt has the following entry in his diary: "Soldiers at WHB have [last night?] cut telephone wires." Though it could be argued that Breithaupt might have lied to Hodgins and Shannon about what the soldiers were doing, the idea that he would have lied to his diary is absurd. The only counter-argument is that this, too, was the work of civilians, which is unlikely. And if one may believe Breithaupt on this point, one is inclined to believe him on others. Cutting phones (and making threatening calls in the middle of the night) was, then, one of the tactics employed by the British League to hinder the campaign of their opponents. And it was a particularly clever one when one remembers that those who opposed the name change avoided public meetings for one reason or another, and that therefore the telephone would have been one of their major means of communication. To have had this disrupted would have made their ability to organize their forces much more difficult.

But much more serious as a cause of lost votes were the "new" regulations governing who had the franchise. These were cleverly established just before voting day, so that even if people had wished to change their status there would have been no time to do so. The effect of these regulations is attested to in several press stories. The *Telegraph*, for example, is typically delighted.

The chief factor in cutting down the opposition vote was the challenging of the alien vote, scores of residents of enemy birth who have lived here for years being unable to vote owing to their being unable to qualify as British subjects. In some cases voters have been in the city for thirty years.

Reports state that over 150 voters were turned away at the polls, though the *Guelph Mercury* stated that about 450 names were cut from the voters' list, and that later another 179 were challenged, so that some 630 residents were disenfranchised. But whether 150 or 630, the numbers certainly explain why the British League emphasized to their Ward committees that they should analyze the voters' lists and have plenty of scrutineers at the polls. This aspect of the campaign was (and still is) particularly galling to those who wished to retain the name. As the later petitioners to the government pointed out,

> the naturalization test was applied strictly to scores of opponents who had lived here for decades, some 40 or even 50 years. They had voted at every parliamentary and municipal election in all these years, and also done jury duty and fulfilled every other function of complete citizens which they had always held themselves to be.

One can certainly sympathize with the bewilderment and exasperation that lies behind this complaint, coming as it does from people who lived in those simpler days when matters of citizenship and naturalization were not much of an issue. One came to a place, one lived there, one worked there, one contributed to its good government, and that was sufficient. Now the ground rules had suddenly changed and they found themselves without a vote and, perhaps even more questionably, without any chance to qualify for a right that was undoubtedly theirs. At best one might say that it was a classic example of a legal injustice. In fact, the campaign as a whole was not fought on a level playing field. If it had been, Berlin would have voted to retain its name by a respectable majority. This is proved by the history of the following six months.

TEN

Kitchener Wins

The following Monday morning Berlin (or Nowhere, Ontario, as one wag suggested the city would have to be called for the time being) witnessed another of its "monster" parades. The 118th Battalion, led by the dignified "Czar," and the less dignified "Collie," now christened "Jake," who went through his usual routine of mindless barking and running around in small circles, was on its way to the G.T.R. station on Victoria Street. Conspicuously absent from the festivities was the man who should properly have presided at them, though his non-attendance was not unexpected. Indeed, the mayor had not been seen since voting day. Some said that it had been made clear to him that his presence would not be welcome on the Saturday when the official farewell took place, and that if he presented the $10 gold pieces the soldiers would refuse to accept them. Cleghorn presided at this function instead, and the coins were handed out by Ed Huber, the city treasurer. Hett later said that the reason he went into hiding until the troops had left was that, quite simply, he was frightened for his physical safety.

Meanwhile, Gallagher, who had been made acting mayor, moved quickly to organize a successful send-off. The schools were given a half-holiday, and all shops and businesses were asked to allow their employees two hours off work. Unfortunately the weather was not under his jurisdiction, and it rained steadily throughout the morning, though this did not stop the citizens from turning out en masse with their umbrellas and giving visible, though damp, expression to the popular war song,

> Oh we don't want to lose you, but we think you ought to go,
> For your King and your Country both need you so.
> We shall want you and miss you but with all our might and main

138

We shall cheer you, thank you, kiss you, tell you come back again.

At the station itself, the band played patriotic or soulful airs, while "mothers clasped sons to their breasts, and sisters and sweethearts dropped tears on rain-wet tunics," and as the first train load pulled out at 9:55 the soldiers, trying for a last hand-shake or hug, leaned out of the windows above what looked like a field of large, black mushrooms; and the air was filled with the sound of the bells of St. Peter's Lutheran Church chiming out "God Be With You Till We Meet Again," "Rule Brittania," and "The Maple Leaf Forever." No doubt there was a broken heart or two, but the only physical casualty occurred when Mayor Hilliard of Waterloo broke his wrist while trying to start his car with a crank handle.

The battalion's final score was 711 officers and men. It was a worryingly low number, but on this emotional day everyone tried to put on a brave face. It was said that recruiting would continue, and it was profoundly hoped that some way would be found of preserving the North Waterloo identity. On the bright side, it was boasted that 65%, or 491, of the enlistments were Canadian-born, which was said to be higher than any other battalion in the Dominion, and 300 of these were of German descent. Where else, asked the *News-Record* could another unit be found in which "Fritz and Tommy marched shoulder to shoulder to uphold British traditions." But now Fritz and Tommy had gone (for the time being anyway) and it was left to the *News-Record* to come out with a valediction of such breath-taking inaccuracy that one searches for the irony. "The entire community regrets their departure. The downtown streets look gloomy and deserted and everyone will miss the good old khaki suits and the happy smiling faces which always adorned the wearers." One wonders whether anyone was unkind enough to remind the newspaper of this passage when those same happy smiling faces smashed up its offices eight months later.

The most pressing need was, of course, to turn Nowhere into Somewhere, and the first moves began almost before the troop trains had disappeared in the direction of London. The citizens were about to discover that getting fixed up with a new name was just about as tricky as discarding an old one. First off the mark was P.V. Wilson, president of the Waterloo Board of Trade, who smartly brought the issue of amalgamation off the shelf where it had been languishing for several weeks. The day after the troops left, he published a long letter in the *Telegraph* outlining all the advantages of such a wedding—that now was the psychological moment; that a suddenly increased population would bring increased prosperity; that outside opinion thought it was a splendid idea; that Waterloo would be bringing to the union a healthy dowry of big insurance companies; that administrative and other costs would be reduced by combining the various public utilities and the municipal government; that they already shared a high school, a hospital, a cemetery, a street railway, and newspapers; that it was absolutely fitting that the chief city of the county should bear the county's name; that the name Waterloo was an honourable one and fulfilled all the patriotic requirements that had been such a feature of the name-change campaign.

With rare unanimity, both the *Telegraph* and the *News-Record* more or less agreed with this proposal. As the former stated, "in all but name and municipal government the two places are already one. Why not consummate the union now." Alas, they had temporarily forgotten what by now should have been fully realized: that a name, with its heavy baggage of identity, history, values and ideals, is a symbol of great power, and therefore has a limitless potential for igniting conflicting passions.

Tuesday night, May 23, was the first meeting of the City Council since the vote. Like one of those dolls that bounces back no matter how hard it is pummelled, Hett was once more in the mayor's chair from whence, exhibiting a good deal more generosity than his opponents, he congratulated them on their victory and made a plea for future peace and harmony. And when he said that he been told that there was a move afoot to demand a recount due to the smallness of the majority, but that he would have nothing to do with such a protest, he heard something he had not heard for weeks: applause.

The main business of the meeting was to resurrect two committees. First there was the Amalgamation Committee which had originally been struck on March 8, and which, after a couple of meetings, had been in abeyance due to the intervention of weightier matters. It was instructed to meet with its Waterloo counterpart on Friday, May 26, in order to make a recommendation to Council. Then there was the name-selection Committee of Ninety-Nine which had been formed on April 3 but had never actually done any work. Now its moment had come, and the various bodies involved were told to have their delegates ready to attend a meeting on Monday, May 29, for the express purpose of coming up with the six names the electorate would be asked to vote on. Any perceptive observer might, perhaps, have foreseen that the seeds of future chaos were contained in the mandates of these two committees because they were potentially pulling in opposite directions. On the one hand the name Waterloo was not on the list to be considered by the Ninety-Nine; on the other, it was well known that Waterloo was fairly committed to the retention of its own name. In the light of existing tensions it was going to be difficult to square this particular circle. To complicate the matter further, one remembers that there was yet a third committee in existence, a "special committee," that had been working away at boiling down the thousands of names to a more manageable number (112 as it turned out) to be considered by the Ninety-Nine. That this committee (Cleghorn, Hahn, Rudell, Hallman, and Master) held convictions and sentiments diametrically opposed to those of the Hetts and Scullys of the Berlin Amalgamation Committee, has already been noted.

The Amalgamation Committees, however, were not unaware of the problem, and initially at least tried to find a way through it. The resolution they agreed on stated that the joint committee

> begs to report that upon careful consideration of the subject, it deems such union feasible and advisable and would respectfully suggest to the Committee of Ninety-Nine the inclusion of the name "Waterloo" for the city amongst those to be voted on, and that the Mayors of the two municipalities be authorized to present this resolution to the said Committee of Ninety-Nine.

Contrary to expectation there was no insistence that Waterloo be the name chosen for the united city. On the other hand it was made clear that *if* another name was chosen, there would be no guarantee that Waterloo would vote for amalgamation.

Thus, when the Committee of Ninety-Nine met on Monday evening, May 29, to consider the 112 names and also to hear the request from the Amalgamation Committees that Waterloo be one of the six final names, the majority weren't sure how to proceed. A minority, however, were well prepared. According to two independent witnesses, while the delegates were still milling about looking for their seats, a voice said, "I move Alderman Hahn take the chair," another voice said, "Seconded," a third said, "Carried," and two seconds later the chair was occupied. This neat piece of railroading took everyone by surprise, and the meeting was underway before anyone thought to object.

Hahn immediately set the tone of the meeting by peremptorily stating that they were there to choose six names suitable for the city, and that it was the duty of the committee to choose the six names from the list in front of them, and that no others, including "Waterloo" would be considered. Period. After a shocked silence, Rev. Spetz, a Roman Catholic priest and a colleague of W.H. Breithaupt's on the Waterloo Historical Board, asked for a clarification, and Hahn repeated the ground rules. Euler politely suggested that as it was well known that many Berlin citizens favoured Waterloo as a name it was only right and proper that they be given a chance to vote on it and that, furthermore, mere courtesy demanded that Mayor Hilliard should be allowed to speak to the resolution. Hilliard did so at some length, reiterating most of the points that Wilson had made in his earlier letter. He was supported by Hett, but Hahn's only reply was, "Can you guarantee that the people of Waterloo will decide to amalgamate after we had voted for the name Waterloo?" Of course no such guarantee could be given, though it was highly likely that they would do so. Hett and Rev. Spetz then presented a resolution that Waterloo be considered by the committee, but Hahn simply declared it out of order. Euler again urged the principle of giving Berlin voters the opportunity of deciding the matter, but Hahn told him that it was against the "rules" of the name contest, and furthermore that to do so would be absurd. If Berliners voted for the name "Waterloo" and then Waterloo turned round and rejected amalgamation they'd all have egg on their faces. He had a point. L.J. Breithaupt then suggested that maybe Waterloo could vote on amalgamation *before* the six names were submitted to the people, but Hahn brusquely dismissed this as too time consuming, and as time was of the essence, "Let's get down to business and boil down these names." At this point Hilliard left the Council chamber.

Attention was then turned to the 112 finalists, and it is to be hoped that at this point a few of the judges experienced some sort of sinking feeling. Some of the rejections have already been noted, but it was still a wretched list. Verbena, Teck, Khaki, Brief, Amity, Arteaga, Cosmos, Uranus, Windigo . . . and so it went on, one ridiculous suggestion after another. If any excuse for the choices can be put forward it is that the original brief had stipulated that no name already on the map could be proposed nor any name connected with past or present wars, names of generals, statesmen, etc. These were severe limitations, but even so one might have expected more imagination and taste. Still, the committee soldiered on through the unwieldy selection process, a dozen yeas being enough to retain a name, and challenges being accepted from all quarters. There were 25 names left for the second round, and 15 for the third. Then everyone was invited to mark their choices 1, 2, 3, 4, 5 and 6, total scores were added up, and the winners were:

> HURONTO
> BERCANA
> DUNARD
> HYDRO CITY
> AGNOLEO
> RENOMA

The reaction was swift and brutal. Nobody (apart from Hahn and his British League cronies, presumably) had anything but contempt for the names, and the phones of the aldermen and the newspapers and the members of the Committee of Ninety-Nine were kept hot with complaints. Even worse for a city that had always been paranoid about outside opinion, the comments in the province's press were uniformly derisive. "Who is taking revenge on the people of Berlin for wanting to have a new name for the city" (*Mail and Empire*); "Why under the sun didn't they put in Onions and Geraniums to fill out the list? Dunard. Sounds like the directions in a quick lunch counter for an order of fried eggs. Renoma. Reno is a place where they get divorces fixed up while you wait, and ma often gets blamed for these. Agnoleo. The last person we came across with that name was perambulating a banana cart" (*Guelph Mercury* — in its less sensitive days); "As the choosing of a new name for Berlin was the work of the 'ninety and nine,' how would 'The Lost Sheep' do?" (*Stratford Herald*); "They looked as if they had been formed by picking letters haphazardly out of a hat" (*Hamilton Spectator*); "They must have been trying to avoid picking one that would prove acceptable" (*Toronto Star*); "If the six names are the best of the many thousands submitted it would be interesting to see the worst six" (*Toronto Globe*).

Hett, surely enjoying the discomfiture of his opponents, wrote to a Toronto legal firm specializing in city names and coats of arms for an expert opinion, and published the reply in the *News-Record*:

> The proceedings of the Committee certainly seem to me to be quite irregular, and further than that I am hardly able to express an opinion.

I have looked over the long list of names in one of the papers and, with the exception of very few not inadmissable [*sic*], there is not a name in the list which is fit for consideration. How a body of sensible men can have given any consideration to such a list is beyond my comprehension.

Of the six names reserved for consideration, five are so undignified that they would be quite unsuitable for an important City. The only one that deserves any consideration whatever is DUNARD, but that is an Irish word, geographically descriptive, and the meaning would be quite inapplicable to your City.

The writer, a certain E.M. Chadwick, added a little cruelly in a postscript, "I notice one name which means an insane murderer or human devil!!!"

But the nicest response, also in the *News-Record*, was the following biblical pastiche:

Huronto, the son of Dunard, called his wife to his side and spake saying: "Agnoleo, the soft whiteness of thy cheek is fairer than the bloom that loves to linger on the lilies of the Nile. Thine eyes are twin thieves, which by some sorcery have ta'en the light from yon poor weeping Waterloo."

And Agnoleo, the wife of Huronto, the son of Dunard made answer: "I care not for thy flattery. I am a jealous woman and love not my neighbour, her name, nor her Ox, nor her Ass, nor anything that is hern (pronounced hahn). But call thou upon Bercana, son of Renoma. And great joy shone forth from the lamps of Bercana whilst Huronto wept.

But it came to pass that a certain man of genius came forth out of the wilderness of Niagara and in a roaring voice cried aloud, "Huronto! Bercana! Dunard! Renoma and Agnoleo! Gather together the rest of your diminutive families and journey with me to Hydro City!" To which command they made swift answer and spake, saying "Let's!"

...Then did Huronto the son of Dunard and Agnoleo, together with Bercana, the son of Renoma become attacked with Hydro-phobia and, falling upon each other's necks, passed in silence out of sight.

Passing silently out of sight was really all that could happen to the inglorious names after such a barrage of laughter, and when the City Council met on Monday, June 5, it politely received the report from the Committee of Ninety-Nine, and then, as the saying goes, filed it.

This Council meeting was essentially a replay of the earlier meeting, hijacked by Hahn, at which the Amalgamation Committees had requested that Waterloo be added to the list of names. Once again Euler and Breithaupt spoke of the advantages of union and once again Hahn objected to the idea, though on this occasion he added a novel argument. Waterloo would actually be an *un*-patriotic choice because it celebrated a victory over a country that was now Canada's ally. Worse than that, it could also be partially viewed as a Prussian success, because of course Blucher had been instrumental in Wellington's victory. It is a pity that he was unable to bring these insights on the mutability of political alliances to bear on current events. But his real objections were also coming more into focus. He was miffed that the smaller municipality seemed to be dictating to the larger. The tail was wagging the dog, as he put it. What he wanted was that both places should drop their names and choose a totally new one. Wrangling on this point followed the first motion put to the meeting: "That if the town of Waterloo immediately submits to a vote the question of amalgamation with this municipality *under the name Waterloo*, this Council agrees that if said vote is favourable to amalgamation the name Waterloo shall be included among those to be submitted to the people of Berlin." The motion was lost, and the meeting turned to other matters, one of which had a certain element of rough justice about it. Hallman presented a bill for the cost of the telegram he had sent to George V on the night of the name-change vote. Gross, as chairman of the Finance Committee, refused payment on the grounds that it hadn't been authorized. Hallman remained $9.00 out of pocket.

Just before adjournment, Schnarr tried for amalgamation once more, with a slightly watered-down version of the earlier motion: "That this Council allow the name Waterloo to be one of the names to be submitted to the Committee of 99, provided the town of Waterloo carry a by-law of amalgamation with this city." The motion was carried, though Hahn was quick to interject, "That don't change anything! The names are still in the hands of the Special Committee!"

But while the aldermen were squabbling over names and amalgamation and the wording of motions, an event had already occurred 4,000 miles away that had a startling and immediate effect on these argumentations. That evening (British time), the armoured cruiser H.M.S. *Hampshire* was battling through a Force 9 gale off the west coast of the Orkneys. It was carrying Britain's Minister of War, Field Marshall Lord Kitchener, on a mission to Russia. At 7:40 p.m. it struck a German mine and went to the bottom in ten minutes. The news came over the wires shortly after the conclusion of the City Council's meeting.

In Britain, the shock that followed the news of Kitchener's death may best be likened to that which followed John F. Kennedy's assassination. In Berlin, Ontario, as in the rest of the Dominion, it was no less. For the British League faction in the name-choice debate it was something of a godsend. To this point they had simply appeared to be pig-headed. A new name had to be found; majority opinion was running in favour of amalgamation with Waterloo; the only alternative names had been dismissed as fatuous. But now, by a stroke of Fate, a name and a cause had suddenly been dropped into their laps. Now they could be pig-headed with a purpose — and never mind the ruling that the names of military leaders were supposed to be ineligible. Furthermore, the reaction as regards the choice of name had been almost instantaneous. Two days later there were two letters in the press suggesting that the new name for the city be Kitchener. One was from a local nurse, Elsie Master, perhaps a relation of the British League alderman, though she doesn't seem to have been quick enough to win the prize. (As far back as February 22, "A Subscriber" had proposed Kitchener's name in a letter to the *News-Record*, and a year before that a strange report in the *London Free Press* stated that a German newspaper had informed its readers that Berlin, Ontario, had been renamed Kitchener.) Within a week city hall had received 200 letters about a new name, 60 percent of them favouring Kitchener, and outside newspapers were echoing the claim made by the *Mail and Empire* that "the new name of Berlin ought to be Kitchener. Upon that there is general agreement."

One way and another, the mine that sank H.M.S. *Hampshire* also sank any hopes of amalgamation. However, the process that had been set in motion had to be tortuously pursued to its inevitable end. On Friday evening, June 9, the Waterloo Council struck an "official" committee to meet with a similar one from Berlin to discuss union. The earlier Amalgamation Committees had apparently been "unofficial." At their Council meeting on Thursday, June 15, Berlin reciprocated by also striking a committee, but it was clear to everyone that negotiations were unravelling fast. The attitude of the British League aldermen was one of amused contempt. A committee could go and talk to Waterloo until it was blue in the face, but as Hahn said, "we wont pay much attention to their report," and as they, to put it bluntly, controlled the Council it was all a bit of a waste of time. Unless, that is, Waterloo got down off its high horse and agreed to meet Berlin on equal terms as regards a name. Presumably, Kitchener.

When the committees met two days later, June 17, Waterloo, no doubt sensing the hardening attitude in their neighbour, elected to raise the stakes by presenting their opposites with the uncompromising resolution that the citizens of Waterloo, "insist that the name must be Waterloo otherwise no by-law will be submitted." If a last straw was need by the Berlin aldermen, this was it. The peremptory tone of "insist" and "must" was noted, and produced the inevitable reaction when Reid and Schnarr introduced their motion calling for amalgamation under the name of Waterloo. Who did this pip-squeak town think it was? And what other gimmicks would they try to force on Berlin when drawing up the terms of agreement? This wasn't amalgamation it was annexation – of the elephant by the mouse. If Waterloo wanted to come and talk business on equal terms, then let them come. Otherwise no deal. Hett and others, desperately hoping that amalgamation could still be salvaged by some less confrontational method, pleaded with Schnarr to withdraw his motion. Hett suggested that a fair solution might be to have two ballots, one containing six names, the other suggesting union under the name Waterloo. That way electors could make their wishes known. But Reid and Schnarr were adamant. They wanted a showdown, and they got it. They were the only two who voted for their motion, and amalgamation was dead.

The only matters left to discuss were the mechanics of the final vote. After some debate it was agreed that the Committee of Ninety-Nine should be laid to rest and that the Council should itself undertake the final selection of names. The 250 names still in the pot had already been whittled down to 30 by Cleghorn's Special Committee, and the Council, dominated of course by the same people, would put forward six of these. "What if the public turn us down?" asked Reid. "They wont," replied Cleghorn. It was agreed that Council should meet again the next day, Wednesday, June 21, to select the six names, and that the voting should start three days later and run for four days in order to give everyone a chance to vote – in other words on June 24, 26, 27, and 28. It was all a bit rushed, but the British League did not want any sort of opposition to materialize.

The selection process took three hours at the Wednesday meeting and was notable only for Gross's heroic attempt to slip Berlin into the list. The suggestion wasted some time, but was unproductive. Only two names received quick approval: Kitchener and Brock. Four more ballots were required to find the other four names, which were clearly only there for window dressing. The final list was:

BROCK
KITCHENER
CORONA
ADANAC
KEOWANA
BENTON

As the four polling days passed, it was noted that electors were not exactly flocking to city hall to cast their ballots. The steam seemed to have gone out of the whole enterprise. According to the *News-Record*, the outstanding feature of the voting was "the absolute indifference displayed by the ratepayers." But the silence they displayed was the silence of exhaustion, or maybe the silence that follows too much frustration and anger. Perhaps it was also the silence of shame. Shortly after 9:00 on June 28, Millar, the city clerk, read out the results to a small crowd of 40 or 50 people. There were no cheers. There was no parade. There were no flags or fireworks. Surprisingly, Kitchener only just came in ahead of Brock, by 346 to 335. In all, 892 ballots were cast, and of these the remarkably high number of 163 were spoiled by those who wrote in Berlin or Waterloo. It was a last sad gesture, for now an alien name had been foisted onto a city whose soul remained unchanged. Berlin had become Kitchener.

ELEVEN

Mopping Up

Though the citizens (or about 8 percent of them anyway) had voted for Kitchener, the name still had to be ratified by Queen's Park, so all was not yet quite lost. During the next two months there was a furious campaign to reverse the decision. Gross, like a dogged sniper covering the retreat of a beaten army, continued to agitate in City Council meetings, and McKay continued to write his convoluted letters to the press. The *News-Record* pointed to the abysmal turnout at the polls and argued that in a matter that was clearly so important to so many people it would be only fair to hold another referendum at a later date when passions had cooled. By "later date" it meant after the next civic elections, and the significance of *that* suggestion was not lost on anybody. The *Telegraph* countered that few people bothered to vote at civic elections anyway so there was no need to get excited at the small turnout. Why, in 1913 only 468 people had voted on a large money authorization for the street railway — all of which had that sliver of truth necessary for disingenuousness. "It has always been recognized," it said, "that 'silence means consent,' and if the electors who did not vote were satisfied to allow others to make the choice of the city's name the selection must necessarily be final."

By the beginning of July a loose grouping of the citizens who had opposed the name change produced a petition with over 2,000 signatures entitled "Statement in Connection with Change of Name of Berlin." Its 14 points detailed the whole history of intimidation, manipulation and disinformation that had characterized the campaign to change the name, and it concluded with a plea for "British fair-play, and a fair review of the question, and especially a consideration of amalgamation with Waterloo as a possible solution of the present difficulty." Even Waterloo

149

County Council got in on the act. At its meeting of July 11, it came out in support of the petitioners, urged postponement of any name change until after the civic elections and passed a resolution suggesting that the two new councils might negotiate union "under either the name of Waterloo or some other name suitable as may be agreed upon." However, Waterloo's own representative rather smugly suggested that his own town was quite comfortable as it was thank you very much and voted against the proposal.

But alas it was all too little too late. If there were 2,000 votes against a name change they should have been marshalled on May 19, intimidation or no intimidation. On July 13 the petitioners met with Premier Hearst. The delegation was as impressive as the one that the British League had mustered on its earlier visits to Queen's Park. W.H. Breithaupt, Scully, Gross, and Mills were of course there, as were Uttley of the *News-Record* and H.M. Bowman and three former mayors, and some captains of industry such as the Langs and Krug and Rumpel. So, too, were Hilliard, Wilson, and McBride from Waterloo. The specific request was that the government delay approval of the name change until after the municipal elections in four months time so that amalgamation with Waterloo could be properly addressed.

The amiable Hearst met them cordially—though one may guess that by now he was muttering his own version of a plague on both your houses—but in the final analysis was unable to give them any offical encouragement. Certainly he agreed with them about amalgamation. "When two towns are so close together," he said, instancing Port Arthur and Fort William, "it is not advisable to duplicate the expense of municipal government," but then this really wasn't an amalgamation issue. It was a name-change issue. "The government gave you an opportunity to settle the question amongst yourselves, and on that score laws have been complied with and votes have been taken." "Under threats and intimidation!" interjected Lang. Hearst shrugged regretfully.

> The government cannot be expected to sit as a court and try those who made threats. You have recourse in other ways. There is the law or, failing that, if you have lost confidence in your City Council you will soon have the opportunity to turn them out.

All of which was depressingly true, and of no use whatsoever in holding back the name change.

But for the next four weeks nothing happened. The government, perhaps still vaguely hoping that tactical inertia would save them from making an unpopular decision, passed no order-in-council authorizing the change of name, and the British League began to get distinctly worried. On Thursday, August 17, they sent deputations to Ottawa and Toronto to try to discover where the holdup lay. One rumour had it that as there was already a Kitchener in British Columbia the Post Office was objecting to the ratification of another one. However, the Postmaster-General assured the Ottawa delegation that this was not so and that they were merely waiting for authorization from Queen's Park. The Toronto delegation discovered what they had indeed suspected: that the Conservative government was very unhappy about the whole thing and was, in effect, dragging its heels. The British League was furious and at a meeting on Friday, August 18, passed the following ultimatum:

> Be it resolved that if the provincial cabinet does not deal favourably . . . with the request of the corporation, not later than Tuesday, August 22, that a monster deputation of citizens of this city wait upon the Government immediately after to demand that the expression of the will of the majority of the electors of this city be respected.

The City Council met on Monday, August 21, to ratify this demand, and it turned into a donnybrook. As usual it was Gross who tried to prevent the passing of the motion. With his sleeves rolled up, and thumping the table, he tried to make himself heard over the roar from the galleries. He yelled at Hett that he wanted the constabulary to be present at the next meeting, but Hett couldn't hear him as he was too busy banging away with his gavel and trying to get five other aldermen to sit down and be quiet. One alderman walked out in disgust. The motion was, of course, passed, and a night lettergram was sent to Queen's Park demanding the ratification of the by-law.

At this point the government had had enough and chucked in the towel. The next morning the city clerk received a call from G.H. Ferguson, the acting attorney-general, requesting the city not to bother with its "monster deputation" as the cabinet would pass the necessary order-in-council that afternoon. Kitchener would become the official name of the city on September 1. The next night, as on May 19, there was the obligatory motorcade, though without the soldiers it somehow lacked fizz. Nor on this occasion did it make a detour to Lang's house. Back at city hall it was Hett who delivered the main speech—for which he received applause. Once again he called for future peace and harmony (though this was not to be for yet awhile) and appealed for sympathy for those who had lost a name that was dear to them and carried many rich associations. At the Council meeting of Monday, August 28, Cleghorn proposed that there be no celebration on the following Friday out of respect for Kitchener's memory. It is doubtful whether he was aware of the irony of making September 1 a day of mourning.

The reluctance of the Breithaupt-Lang forces to organize themselves into a militant public body was, as has been suggested, a major reason why they lost the name of their city. Having lost it, they finally realized that they would have to come out of the closet, or else continue to allow a strident minority to manipulate civic affairs. On Thursday, August 24, the day after the order-in-council accepted Kitchener as the new name, some 200 citizens met at the Borden Club and created the Citizens' League. The first principle of its manifesto stated that "the League shall be non-political," but this was obviously not going to be true in a civic sense. The *Telegraph* was being more accurate when it called it "an organization to elect a municipal council at the forthcoming elections," though when it went on to claim that such a council intended "to submit another by-law to wipe Kitchener off the Canadian map and restore Berlin," it was reporting a Citizens' League policy that was still under debate. At the inaugural meeting both Breithaupt and Uttley, for example, called for union with Waterloo, though Gross stoutly maintained that he wanted the old name back again. And it was Gross who was the star of the meeting. Every speaker acknowledged the lonely and, indeed, dangerous battle that he had been waging in Council over the past year, and when he rose to speak he received a standing ovation.

> You and I who were born here as British subjects had a right to express our opinion on the name of Berlin and had a right to a wish to retain it. Gentlemen, I'd sooner die than submit to the dictates of a few. We should not let the matter drop. I believe we should consider whether we could not take out an injunction and try to delay the change.

Over the next three months Breithaupt's moderation softened his views.

The executive of the new League contained many familiar names. August Lang was president, Reid was vice-president, and Scully was treasurer. On the executive and the committees were J.R. Eden and W.H. Schmalz, both former mayors, Breithaupt, John Lang, A.L. Bitzer, Uttley, and H.M. Bowman, the author of an earlier pamphlet arguing against the name change. It was further agreed that meetings would be held on the second and fourth Thursdays of each month.

As the weeks passed, the confidence of the Citizens' League grew. Their meetings were packed, and they had to move into ever larger halls. With popularity came an increasing robustness. Like schoolchildren suddenly discovering that it was safe to stick their tongues out at the playground bully, they began to enjoy their newly acquired freedom, and the bigwigs of the British League found that they had lost their monopoly on personal insults. At their meetings and in the *News-Record*, their semi-official organ, the likes of Cleghorn, Hahn, and Williams were given the sort of treatment that they had been handing out to others. "Since Alderman Hahn has taken such an active part in changing the city's name, claiming it was too German for him, he should change his own name, which is a German one. Anglicized it would be 'Rooster.'" One way and another the silent majority was becoming vocal, and undoubtedly one of the reasons for this was the (temporary) absence of the British League's enforcers, the men of the 118th, who were currently choking on the dust of Camp Borden. Indeed, strange and disturbing stories were filtering in from time to time about the boys in khaki at their summer camp. There were even rumours about officers staging a revolt. Something to do with lack of discipline, though this wouldn't have come as much of a surprise to the folks back home. Later the even more interesting news filtered through that Lochead had been given a "promotion" to District Assistant Quartermaster General, which sounds a bit like inviting a quarterback to be in charge of the orange juice — though perhaps the position was more important than that when one remembers Napoleon's dictum about an army marching on its stomach. Whatever the truth of all this, the important point was that the 118th Battalion played no part in the current civic election campaign — until it was too late to affect the outcome.

The campaign itself followed the expected format of good, dirty fun, though heightened this time as both sides were fighting on equal terms, and any tit could expect to receive a fair amount of tat. It was in effect a rerun of the first name-change vote, and as polling day came closer the issue of who should or should not be on the voters' lists once again became crucial. However, on this occasion there was plenty of lead time, and the Citizens' League was able to make provision for registering their supporters. This skirmish came to a head on Friday, December 16, when the two sides appeared before Judge Hanning in the Court of Revision to register or appeal against names on the voters' list, Certainly a large enough number, 593 citizens, were involved to influence the outcome of the election (and perhaps giving us a fair idea of how many were disenfranchised in the earlier name-changing vote), but the Citizens' League was well prepared. They were represented by Bowman and Bitzer, while Hahn and Heisey appeared for the British League. The latter drew first blood when Hahn claimed that Bowman himself shouldn't be on the voters' list as he wasn't a householder, and when Bowman couldn't immediately prove the contrary, Judge Hanning insisted that he produce his lease. Fortunately he was able to do this the following day. At the end of the session the British League had managed to get some 100 residents struck from the list, which was far fewer than had been debarred earlier. Furthermore, their opponents had now learnt how to play the political game, and they immediately published the names of those "who were deprived of their franchises by the action of the British League last week" along with the number of years they had lived in the city. Thus: "George Allendorf, 30 years; Fred Ackernecht, 23 years; Moritz Bastion, 34 years," and so on. It was an impressive roll call, and no doubt the resentment it generated did much to make the British League's tactics counter-productive.

On Saturday, December 17, the "largest crowd in the history of the city" packed the Star Theatre for the nominations to the various municipal offices. Considering that equal numbers of British League and Citizens' League supporters were present, it was a remarkably peaceful meeting, though there were rumbles of discontent when the intransigent referred to the city as "Berlin," and when Gross stated that, "Legally the name is Kitchener but in my heart it is still Berlin." Hett opened the meeting with a valedictory address ("I think you will agree these have been two strenuous years" [cat calls and applause])" in the course of which he explained that he hadn't attended the celebrations when the vote to change the name was passed on May 19 because he believed his life was in danger (considerable laughter). The nominations proceeded, and they came in record numbers. There were 15 for mayor, 47 for the Council, and 27 for the various Commissions. However, everyone knew that the two Leagues would be streamlining their slates within a few days.

The final Council meeting before the election was on Monday, December 19, and was a "disorderly row." No one was quite sure what it was all about, but the *Telegraph* was probably correct when it stated that

> the only reason that can be assigned for the unseemly rumpus is that the aldermen who participated in it realized that it was the last meeting of the year and they were loath to lose an opportunity to give vent to the wrath that had been rankling in their hearts since the start of the name-changing controversy.

Hahn and Gross were, of course, the ringleaders, with Hett furiously telling Hahn to sit down and threatening to have the police come and eject him, and Hahn telling him to go right ahead, and Gross marching about with clenched fists saying that he'd do the job himself, and some ladies of the Daughters of the Empire in the galleries departing in alarm — all of which made for a spectacle that, as the *Telegraph* suggested, was reminiscent of one of the ridiculous campaign scenes in *The Pickwick Papers*.

On Friday, December 22, the British League published their slate of candidates. For mayor: W.E. Gallagher; for Aldermen: Cleghorn, Hahn, Detweiler, Ferguson, Hessenauer, Kaufman, Knechtel, Master, Rose, Rudell, and Schnarr.

On Tuesday, December 26, The Citizens' League put forward their slate. For mayor: David Gross; for aldermen: Asmussen, Bitzer, Bowman, Brubacher, Campbell, Gofton, Huehnergard, Iler, McKay, Ratz, Reid, Sass, Schwartz, Zettel, Uttley.

It was to be a head-to-head contest, with the two sides sporting most of the major participants of the earlier battles. Tactically it was a clever move by the British League to choose Gallagher as their mayoral candidate. He was something of a moderate, and as a former Trades and Labour Council man he would be attractive to the working-class vote. But the Citizens' League perhaps had an even better icon in the fiery Gross, who represented in his person unwavering opposition to the name-changers and their autocratic ways. The names of the aldermen speak for themselves. For the most part they divide as they had divided on the floor of the Council chamber and in the press over the past year. It is also worth noting that the British League only fielded 11 candidates, which may have been an early sign of weakness.

In the last days before the election, the British League continued to exploit the fear that their opponents intended to change the name back to Berlin if they won (though this wouldn't have aroused much fear in the hearts of many), while the Citizens' League maintained a careful ambiguity on the issue. After nine platitudinous clauses, its "Platform" concluded with a statement clearly designed to attract both the the militants and the moderates amongst its followers: "as true Britishers, we are opposed to the introduction of the name controversy as an issue at this election or as long as we require the united effort of our people to prosecute the war to a successful conclusion." Robert Bourassa could not have put it better. At the Citizens' League's final rally at Victoria Hall on December 29, Gross made no mention of the matter. In his audience that night there were some familiar faces. A large contingent of the 118th, recently arrived for the Christmas season, was back in town. Doubtless they were trying on their old intimidation tactics, but the days when that might have worked were over. Now, heavily outnumbered, they were easily cowed into silence and, indeed, Gross cheerfully noted their presence and said how pleased he was to see them. Events three days later were to offer them a better opportunity for bullying.

Voting was much heavier on New Year's Day, 1917, than it had been on May 19 for the name change, and though trouble was expected there was none while the polls were open. The Citizens' League had taken a leaf out of their opponents' book, and were well organized with ward committees and scrutineers and cars to get their supporters to the polls. The soldiers were in evidence but had had no time to organize any effective intimidation. This time, too, the military authorities had finally been persuaded to take precautionary measures. Major Osborne, Assistant Provost Marshall, had been sent from London along with three military policemen to keep an eye on events, and on top of that a detachment of the 122nd Battalion stationed in Galt was placed on stand-by duty in case of serious rioting.

The polls closed at 5:00, and by 6:30 the first returns were in from Poll 3 in the North Ward. Gallagher 26; Gross 110. Over the next hour or so this pattern was repeated. Even in the East Ward, which had been a British League stronghold on May 19, three of the six polls went for Gross, and another was tied. By 7:30 the size of the Citizens' League victory had become apparent. It was as comprehensive a rout of the British League as one could expect. Gross finally polled 2,052 votes to Gallagher's

1,298. The results of the aldermanic race were even more startling. It was a clean sweep for the Citizens' League nominees. Not a single British League candidate was elected. Cleghorn was out, Rudell was out, Schnarr was out. Hahn came second from the bottom. A more comprehensive rejection of the arrogant and divisive jingoism that had ruled in the city for the past year cannot be imagined. It is also the clearest proof that had the earlier election been conducted fairly the name would not have been changed.

But the evening was far from over. If the British League and its khaki supporters had shown themselves to be ungracious winners on May 19, it was nothing to how they behaved as losers. At about 8:00 a jubilant crowd had gathered inside and outside the *News-Record* office, just down from the Walper House, watching the returns being posted, when along King Street came the boys of the 118th, led by none other than Sergeant Major Granville Blood. Inevitably, insults began to be traded back and forth, and then the soldiers began to push into the office. Here verbal attempts were made to defuse the situation, but to no avail. The shouting quickly escalated into shoving, and when a plate-glass window went, the riot started. Two aldermen-elect, Nick Asmussen and W.H. Bowman, got involved in the fisticuffs and were beaten up. It was thought that the latter had been seriously injured, but this turned out not to be the case.

At this moment, Major Osborne was down the road at city hall informing Police Chief O'Neill that his military police had heard rumours that the *News-Record* office was going to be "cleaned up" (read "wrecked"). A minute or two later Uttley rushed in with the same information. But before a rescue operation could be organized, a bloody-faced Asmussen staggered in with the news that the riot had already started. He was quickly followed by Gross, who told him that a party of soldiers had been looking for him at his house on Water Street. Osborne informed Gross that "it was absolutely necessary that under the circumstances he go to some friend's house . . . and there keep quiet and let no one know of his whereabouts." Osborne who, if his report is anything to go by, was a fussy, self-important, self-justifying military windbag of the worst sort, went down to the *News-Record*'s offices, cleared it and put two military police on duty. He then phoned Hett to come down to King Street to have a look at the situation, but Hett was too scared, so they arranged to meet at city hall instead. Back at city hall Osborne found Hett

> very undecided as to the course of action to take. In fact I might state, that none of the civil officials seemed to know what they should do, or what action to take, and constantly referred to me for advice, and seemed to be totally unable to come to any decision as to what they should do under such circumstances. Mr. Uttley was insisting upon protection. Finally the mayor told me that he requested military protection. I told him he would have to make a request in the official manner, when his request would be immediately complied with. He made this request officially, which I here attach.

The situation was now getting serious, and Osborne sent an urgent call to Galt to get the 122nd Battalion to Kitchener as quickly as possible. It was on its way by 10 o'clock and arrived an hour later.

While Osborne was watching Hett dither, and making him write out official requests, and generally huddling with the civic authorities at city hall waiting for help, the rioters returned to the attack on the *News-Record*. While some shoved past the military guard at the front of the building, others broke in the back and began to wreck the presses, smash doors and windows, toss furniture out into the street and generally repeat the Concordia escapade. They had the run of the downtown area for about an hour, but at last the Galt troops arrived. They immediately formed fours in preparation for a march down King Street, headed by Osborne and, at his insistence, a no doubt terrified Hett. However, they had got no further than Frederick when they were confronted by a mob in a distinctly ugly mood. The Galt troops were ordered to fix bayonets. The situation was now on the knife edge of a genuine disaster. In his report Osborne states,

> I immediately realized that if I allowed them to surround my party I would become absolutely powerless. I therefore formed line at this point and blocked King Street, and prevented further passage of the crowd. They came quite close to the soldiers and appeared to be in a very angry mood. I called upon the people to retire. I waited a few moments and again repeated the order. I saw that determination was required, in order to impress upon them that I was there on serious business and intended to carry it out. . . . For the third time I called upon the people to disperse, and told them it was my intention to move on down King Street. . . .

I again addressed the mayor personally, in a quiet tone, and told him it was my intention to move at a slow pace down King Street. . . . I again reminded him that he would, if necessary, have to read the Riot Act, when he remarked that at that time he saw no riot, which in a sense was true. But the people would not obey, and did not seem disposed to move. I brought my men, after cautioning them, to the position of the charge, when the people gradually moved back. At a very slow and steady pace I then moved on down King Street, the people gradually retiring in front of my men.

On arriving at Queen Street I threw a cordon across that point, so blocking up that portion of the street. I then moved on and blocked up King Street where Foundry crosses, and then proceeded with the assistance of the civil police to clear the people from the intervening space between Queen and Foundry, quietly passing them through the cordon of soldiers blocking up these points. I found considerable difficulty in getting the people to obey. They did not seem to realize the seriousness of the situation or the observance of authority.

Having cleared the streets, Osborne set heavy guards on the *News-Record* office, and Gross's house and button factory, and the night passed without further incident. The next day the men of the 118th Battalion were rounded up, their passes were confiscated, and they were shipped off back to London. Amongst those seeing them off was a group of ultra-patriotic army wives, led by Lil Garner, who was by now "well known to the police authorities." The crowd was still in a state of ferment from the previous day's events and looking for any excuse for a spot more aggravation. As they were coming down Foundry Street, Lil espied the unfortunate Reid, the newly elected Citizens' League alderman, and therefore one of the "enemy." After a few verbal sallies, she started throwing snowballs at him, but when this didn't seem to be effective attacked him with her fists. Reid grabbed a hockey stick to defend himself, but a soldier, with misplaced gallantry, disarmed him. Reid made off in confusion, followed by the victorious jeers of Lil and her tricoteuses, who then continued on down King Street to see if they could sniff out more trouble.

During the day the *News-Record* replaced its plate-glass window, but late that night another brick was tossed through it by a hit-and-run soldier. A constable saw the incident and set off in pursuit. The soldier darted into a café, and the constable, confident that he had cornered his man, darted in after him. The café was filled with about 30 soldiers. The constable darted out again. This was the final incident of the civic election campaign, and with it (though he tells it slightly differently) Osborne more or less concludes his report. His last paragraph, perhaps the crowning example, of the many that we have seen, of military obtuseness, is worth quoting: "Finally, I may state positively that during my tour of duty in the City of Kitchener, I had no evidence that the men of the 118th Battalion, or any other men in uniform, had any part in the disturbance, and, as far as I could learn, were in no way responsible for it."

There were high expectations at the first meeting of the new Council on Monday morning, January 8, though of what nobody quite knew. Would there be an announcement that the name would be changed back to Berlin? Would there be an uproar? Maybe even a riot? Amongst the spectators were the British League's losing candidates, but it was also noted that, now that he was in a position to do so, Gross had ordered the attendance of the police. There was one at each entrance to the gallery and another guarding the entrance to the councillors' area. Sitting conspicuously at a side table was Major Osborne, back again from London to keep an eye on a potentially tricky occasion. But he and the spectators and the police, and the two reporters from Toronto with their quick-sketch artist, were to be disappointed. Gross's short inaugural address was all to do with good government, fiscal responsibility, and so on, and then right at the end he referred to the matter that was uppermost in everyone's mind. "I believe I may say for you as I say for myself that there will not be any proposal to rechange the name of the city during the life of this Council." This probably disappointed some of the diehards, of which Gross himself had been one, but there was, of course, no other policy that could reasonably have been pursued. To have subjected the city once again to months of horrific turmoil was quite out of the question. Wounds now had to be healed, and though many, if not the majority, of the citizens would have to live with their regrets for a time, these too would eventually fade away. In December 1919 there was, in fact, one more attempt to change the name back to Berlin, and aldermen such as Bitzer, Bowman, and Asmussen were roughed up by the mob, and the *News-Record* was again smashed up, but Kitchener remained Kitchener and that was the end of it.

On a global scale the civil war in Berlin, Ontario, in 1916 hardly bears comparison with more ferocious arguments such as those currently being waged between Arabs and Jews, or Serbs and Croats, or Irish Catholics and Protestants. But it is possible for small dogfights to illuminate larger ones, and such is the case here. For example, the origins and pressures and alignments of such contests are always a lot more complex than the popular wisdom of slogans and newspaper headlines make them out to be. The battle for Berlin's name is often thought to have been mainly a contest between the "British" and the "Germans." This was obviously not the case for, as has been seen, as many "Germans," that is, people with German-sounding names, fought to change the name as to retain it, and to find out why they took this side or that side one would need to know whether particular "Germans" had just arrived or were third generation, were from Bavaria or Thuringia, or even Austria or Switzerland, whether they had left their country happily or with regret, and so on. Conversely, a significant number of "British" people fought hard to retain the name—the McKays and Scullys, the Reids and Edens and Campbells and Kingsleys. Complicating the ethnic factor was the factor of class. The inherent distrust of the worker for the boss was a significant element of both the recruiting and name-change campaigns, and one that boiled vividly to the surface in the Trades and Labour Council's attack on recruiting methods in January 1915. But here again divisions were blurred. Lochead may have been president of the Board of Trade and Reid president of the Trades and Labour Council, but Krug, Rumpel, and Lang were Board of Trade members, while Gallagher was one of the "workers." Perhaps in the final analysis it is the individual human character that cuts across and modifies both class and ethnicity, and fixes ultimate allegiances. Thus in all partisan struggles, such as the one we have been looking at, there are those who are guided mainly by reason and understanding and the spirit of compromise and those who are shortsighted and easily swayed by cheap emotionalism. Berlin in 1916 was a microcosm of the shrill patriotism that was endemic to most countries in World War I. In this Ontario city it was, perhaps, more focussed, intense, and outrageous than it was elsewhere, and for that reason it illustrates with more than usual clarity the truth of Samuel Johnson's dictum that patriotism is the last refuge of the scoundrel.

Epilogue

This episode of Kitchener's history has been a fascinating mixture of tragi-comedy, farce, and theatre of the absurd, but before ringing down the curtain let us briefly note, for the curious reader, the tales of a few of the major players and the outcome (or lack of it) of one or two of the subjects.

Who, for example, won the glittering prizes in the Name That City Contest? It was not, after all, Elsie Master, or "Subscriber," or even an unknown German journal, but Miss Lillian Spears of Toronto, Miss Sadie Powers of Brantford, and Miss Clavis Harrington of Toronto. The first won $133.33, the second $50.00, and the third $16.67. Unfortunately the city had only been able to collect $200 instead of the promised $300, and the new City Council had refused to make up the difference. Cleghorn, who was still in charge of the relevant committee, was thus able to get in one last hurrah. He sent the cheques to the winners with an explanation of the shortfall, and concluded, "I am sorry that I have to refer you to the Kitchener City Council for the balance of the prize money."

Hett, though he emerges from this story with considerable honour, had a questionable career later on. He threw his hat into the ring of provincial politics in 1917 and 1929, both times without success. He moved his medical practice to Windsor where he concentrated more and more on cancer cures. These cures, which he dispensed to many hopeful sufferers, were, to be generous, of a dubious nature. Indeed, he was struck off the medical register in 1937 and 1952 when he resisted independent analysis of his secret serum. He died of a stroke in Windsor in 1956 at the age of 75.

Lochead had a quiet war. When he came to be assessed for overseas service, the reports were mixed. According to Patricia

162

McKegney, General Lessard considered him "energetic and willing to learn," but lacking in military experience. Colonel Shannon essentially agreed, and added that he was "not regarded as a good disciplinarian," which could only have come as a surprise to the army. Lochead went with the remnant of his battalion to England, but when it was broken up he was assigned to the 25th Reserve Battalion at Bramshott. He remained there for six months and was then honourably discharged. He returned home to command his old home guard unit, the 108th Regiment, and to continue his job with Mutual Life at their head office in Waterloo. He was prominent in fraternal organizations becoming, for example, a 33rd degree Mason, and potentate of the Mocha Temple. He died at St. Mary's Hospital, Kitchener, at the age of 86 in 1960.

During the war Sergeant Major Blood became a sapper, but no details are known of his service. When he returned he joined the Ontario Provincial Police, and during prohibition was a fearless pursuer of bootleggers. The story goes that his last operation was to apprehend, single-handedly, a gang operating in a swamp near the Formosa Brewery. He was found the next morning badly beaten and paralyzed. For a short time he was a caretaker at the Canadian Legion. In the 1960s he was still living with his wife, Agnes, at 48 Locust Street in Kitchener, the same house that he had occupied since before the Great War. His last years were unhappy. One neighbour recalls that he had often seen a tattered figure shuffling along King Street with a canvas bag over one shoulder – a ghost revisiting the scene of past glories? – and being surprised when he learnt that the man was Sgt. Blood and that he lived on the same street. Around 1970, Blood suffered a stroke, and when shortly afterwards Agnes went into hospital, local ladies voluntarily took him meals. They found him not an agreeable person, but the miseries of age and sickness temper such a judgment. He was transferred to a veterans' hospital in London and died in 1973 at the age of 88. One citizen who remembers those far-off days claims that he still has his memorial in the city he helped to terrorize. In the old English Tract just south of Schneider's there is a short street of modest houses. It bears the name Grenville Street, but as Blood spelt his Christian name with an 'a' the attribution seems unlikely. The belief, however, persists. He is buried in Woodland Cemetery in Kitchener.

Gross served three consecutive terms as mayor, and continued to operate the Dominion Button Manufacturers on Water

Street until it was taken over by his son. He became ill in 1944, and went to the Mayo Clinic where he died under surgery aged 78. The button factory, unable to compete with cheap imports, was closed in 1964. It is now the site of the Alexandrian Apartments.

W.H. Breithaupt who, with Gross, could be considered one of the two heroes of this story, continued to work as an engineer and also to participate in civic government. He was the first chairman of the City Planning Commission from 1917 to 1921. But perhaps his first love was the heritage of his city and county. He became the first president of the Waterloo Historical Society, a position he retained for 12 years, and helped to organize the building of the Memorial Tower to commemorate the early pioneers. He worked hard to imporve the library, and pioneered the Grand River Conservation Authority. He died in 1944 at the age of 86.

After leaving Berlin, Tappert became pastor of St. Luke's Church in New Rochelle, New York. The small congregation that he served there, and in nearby Mamaroneck, where the services were held in an abandoned schoolhouse, was a far cry from the spacious St. Matthew's, where he had preached to upwards of 1,000 people. In 1924 he was invited to become editor of *Lutherischer Herold*, the German weekly publication of the United Lutheran Church. He remained in this position until 1943, when he was 77. He died in Philadelphia on March 22, 1948, at the age of 83. His grandchildren still live in New Rochelle, and also in Calgary. They feel no rancour towards the city that maltreated their ancestor.

Private Joe Meinzinger of the quick fists became mayor of Kitchener in 1940. And in 1941, '42, '43, '44, '45, '59, '61, and '62. Still remembered by many residents of Kitchener, he appears to have remained the quintessential rough diamond to the end, either loved or hated, depending on whether one had opposed his will or not. He died in 1962 at the age of 70 and at his funeral, which was one of the largest the city had witnessed, Msgr. Haller suggested that "had he been born today he would have been called a juvenile delinquent" but that "even with all his faults and failures there was a certain respect he demanded. He was a wonderful man, unique in every way, with no sign of hypocrisy." His old sparring mate, Jim Blevins, continued in the city's police force and eventually became its most famous detective. A later photograph shows a face, complete with tilted-down trilby, that Bogart might have studied for some role as a Chandler detective. Blevins's most famous exploit was in 1941. After a robbery at the Bank of Commerce in St. Clements he pursued the criminals for eight miles, blazing away from the car window in the best movieland tradition. He died of a heart attack in 1948 while visiting a daughter in Toronto. He was 71.

Hahn died in 1960 at the age of 84. In spite of his ambitions he never rose to the highest public offices. He became an alderman again in 1923, and in 1927 he was clerk of the Waterloo County Council. Subsequently he was the manager of the Kitchener Liquor Control Board.

The fate of the 118th Battalion was suitably ignominious. After spending the summer of 1916 at Camp Borden it was sent back to London, now reduced to two companies. In January 1917, the remaining 540 men were subjected to a rigorous medical inspection, and nearly half of them were found to be unfit, due to flat feet and other ailments. At the end of January, 246 set off for England. Most were seasick and their ship ran aground off Liverpool. At Bramshott camp they were put into a reserve battalion and subsequently dispersed into other units. The 118th was officially disbanded on August 4, 1917.

The mystery of the Kaiser's bust remains unresolved. At the court of inquiry after the Concordia Club riot the interrogating officers clearly tried very hard to establish where the bust had got to. They particularly grilled Wilkins, the Corporal of the Guard, and Gough, the Provost Corporal. The latter admitted to putting the bust in the detention room "to keep the fellows from smashing it up." The door was opened once more, because Blood said he wanted to have a look at it. The next morning, when the door was unlocked around 7:30, it was gone. Gough's evidence at this point has an aura of truth about it.

Q: When did you first open the detention room this morning?
A: Just after I had my breakfast.
Q: And who got the bust then?
A: There was no bust there. There were three or four more fellows wanted to see it and I took them in to see it and when I got in it was gone.
Q: Where was the key?
A: In my pocket in my pants, and I rolled them up and slept on them.
Q: Any other keys?
A: Yes, two more. I asked him (Sgt. Pawson) about it this morning, and he said he turned two keys in.

Q: There are other men here in quarters who know you carry the key?

A: Yes sir.

Q: Do you suppose they would remove it?

A: They could not take my key. I can swear my key never left my ring, as I always keep on my pants.

Q: You don't know where the bust is now?

A: No sir.

Q: Who was the first man who asked about the bust this morning?

A: We were talking about the bust this morning. One of the men said, "has the Kaiser had his breakfast?" I said, "No, and we'd better take him some in."

Q: And that is the first you knew the bust was gone?

A: Yes sir.

Q: Who else came around?

A: They all flocked in.

Q: Did any of the Machine Gun men go in?

A: Yes sir, they all came in. They were mad.

Q: Why should they be mad?

A: Because they said they wanted to take it up to their room last night.

Q: Why should they be interested in it at all? Do you think they have any particular interest in the bust?

A: I could not tell. They seemed to be the fellows who wanted it.

Clearly the officers had no idea where the bust was, and a number of the soldiers didn't either, and were, indeed, quite put out that they had been deprived of their trophy. Assuming that it would have been impossible for civilians to undertake a rescue operation, it follows that a small group of soldiers (presumably it would have required two or three to carry the bust) got hold of one of the spare keys and spirited it away during the night. It is also interesting that whoever masterminded the operation was senior enough to get it organized (one cannot imagine three or four privates pulling off such a heist) and astute enough to realize that the bust had to disappear that very night. To have allowed it to remain on display as an object of derision, the more obvious and popular choice, would almost certainly have meant that the authorities would have confiscated it, and eventually returned it to the Concordia Club.

As to where the bust ended up, one story says it was buried (and still is) in a back garden on Yonge Street but this has the Arthurian tinge to it of the sleeping hero. Another suggests that it was taken to a foundry, of which there were certainly a sufficient number in the city, and there melted down into table napkin rings. However, one may object that there wouldn't have been a great number of foundries open at 10 o'clock at night, and a priority must have been to get the bust hidden as quickly as possible. Perhaps it was smuggled to the house of one of the N.C.O.'s, several of whom lived out of barracks, though it is unlikely that it was carried very far (Blood's house, for example, was too far away) for fear of being observed. Interestingly enough, Sergeant Pawson, who at one time had keys to the detention room, happened to live right next door, at 34 Courtland East. There was even a handy lane from the barracks to his back garden. Maybe it was stored here for a while and later melted down.

Two stories in the *Kitchener-Waterloo Record* (September 20, 1956; October 4, 1966) purport to tell what happened next. They claim that the bust was hidden amongst the battalion's baggage when it went to Carling Heights training camp in London, and it was there that "the bust was melted down, its metal rolled into sheet, and formed into napkin holders." These were then distributed and hence "scattered throughout the country." However, several questions remain unanswered. Though it is possible that the bust could have been smuggled out of the city amongst the military baggage without the officers knowing about it, one would have thought that it would have been easier to have had it melted down in Berlin, where there would have been closer contacts with local foundries, than in a relatively strange city. Secondly, a lot of napkin holders could be made from a 200-pound bust, but as yet only one has surfaced. It is at Doon Pioneer Village and is listed as "reputed to be" from the bust. It is essentially a strip of metal bent over into a flattish U-shape, on one side of which is soldered a 118th badge, probably originally a cap badge. The file card of this artefact lists no donor and no date, and those who might be expected to know such things have no recollection of how or when it was acquired. The first *Record* story claims that it originally came from a Toronto woman "who prefers to remain anonymous," the second that it was donated by "an ex-officer of the 118th Batallion [*sic*]" who "prefers to remain unidentified." Finally, it is strange that no more of these rings have come to light. If there were so many of them quite a few must surely have ended up in local "battalion" hands, and it is difficult to see why there would now be any further need for secrecy. A cursory check at the War Museum in Ottawa, and other military museums, has turned up no more napkin holders. The puzzle remains an intriguing one.

Finally, there is the issue of the amalgamation of the cities of Kitchener and Waterloo, an idea that remains as unlikely as it is obvious. As has been recounted, the reasons for turning it down in 1916 were almost purely irrational. The Amalgamation Committees concluded that there were no economic disadvantages, to the contrary, but the rancour and sheer mulishness of the main players, even before the death of Kitchener, was enough to scuttle it. In Berlin, the very fact that those who were against the name change were the ones who were pressing for the compromise of amalgamation was sufficient reason for the other side to oppose it. Irrational enmity could not be taken much further. In Waterloo, there was never any serious thought given to surrendering the city's name. Any new, united city would have to be called Waterloo, or there was no deal. This, and indeed the whole fight to retain the name Berlin, illustrates the emotional potency of names. Names, after all, are important no matter what Juliet thought. To be deprived of a name is to be deprived of identity and history, and like a bereavement the loss will be felt until Time or substitutes or restitution fill in the gap.

But perhaps the supreme irony in the whole affair lies in the changed perceptions about the name that was lost and the name that was gained. Berlin, though it may still elicit anger in the breasts of those still living 50 years in the past, is now as likely to be associated with reunification or Checkpoint Charlie, or perhaps seen as the most important city in the modern European Community. Kitchener, on the other hand, seems to be primarily known as a successful imperialist general whose main campaigns involved mowing down the fuzzy wuzzies (as Kipling would have it) with maxim guns, and inventing concentration camps for Boer women and children. The name wouldn't stand a chance in a modern vote.

Since 1916 there have been several attempts to unite the two cities, the last being in 1970 when the Fyfe report strongly recommended such a move. An overwhelming 83 percent of Waterloo's citizens rejected the proposal. According to Ken McLaughlin in *Waterloo: An Illustrated History*, Fyfe "was astonished" at this result, but consoled himself with the prediction that "it is only a matter of time before an amalgamation takes place" (pp. 111-12). Time will tell. Meanwhile it is true that, as McLaughlin goes on to state, "despite outward similarities,

Waterloo had always been different from Kitchener. Although close geographically, there had long been a dramatic difference in the temperament and operation of the two cities." This observation is borne out by an impressionistic stroll down their respective downtown cores, neither of which are, at present, marvellously attractive. Both have their share of garish store fronts behind which can still be glimpsed the façades of older buildings, and Waterloo even has an extensive car park fronting a large portion of its main street. But Waterloo also has space, and therefore room for trees and flower beds along its sidewalks, while Kitchener's core (to end up where we began) seems cramped and airless. Space and trees. Perhaps these are the outward and visible signs of inner, invisible reasons why these two cities are far from being identical twins, and why, though they share schools and hospitals and cemeteries and transport systems, their respective citizens sense that they live in different places.

Not so many years ago a friend went into a Waterloo hardware store to buy a replacement for some attachment or other that had broken off a crib. The clerk looked at it and shook his head pessimistically. No, they didn't have one, and hadn't had one in some time. Had he tried the other stores in town. Yes. Well then, all he could suggest was going to Toronto for it, or maybe sending for it, but that might take a few weeks. The friend was about to leave when the clerk suddenly stopped him. "There is one other possibility," he said. "Do you ever get down into Kitchener?"

Bibliography

Books, Articles, and Personal Papers

Berlin, Celebration of Cityhood, 1912. Berlin: German Printing and Publishing Co., 1912.

Berlin Today, 1806-1906, Centennial Number in Celebration of the Old Boys' and Girls' Reunion. Berlin: News-Record, 1906.

Breithaupt, L.J. "Diary," in the Breithaupt papers held in the Doris Lewis Rare Book Room, University of Waterloo.

Breithaupt, W.H. "Diary," in the Breithaupt papers held in the Doris Lewis Rare Book Room, University of Waterloo.

Bricker, I.C. "The History of Waterloo Township up to 1825." *Waterloo Historical Society Records* 22 (1934): 81-122.

Busy Berlin: One of the Greatest Industrial Centres of Ontario. Berlin: S.n., n.d.

Capon, Alan R. *His Faults Lie Gently: The Incredible Sam Hughes.* Lindsay: Floyd W. Hall, 1969.

Day, Cindy. "Anti-German Sentiment in Berlin During the First World War." Waterloo: S.n., 1988.

Dunham, Mabel. *Grand River.* Toronto: McClelland & Stewart, 1945.

English, John, and McLaughlin, Kenneth. *Kitchener: An Illustrated History.* Waterloo: Wilfrid Laurier University Press, 1983.

Eksteins, Modris. *Rites of Spring: The Great War and the Birth of the Modern Age.* London: Transworld Publishers, 1989.

Epp, Frank H. *Mennonites in Canada, 1786-1920: The History of a Separate People.* Toronto: Macmillan, 1974.

Horst, Isaac R. *Up the Conestogo.* 1979.

McKegney, Patricia P. *The Kaiser's Bust.* Bamberg: Bamberg Press, 1991.

McLaughlin, Kenneth. *Waterloo: An Illustrated History.* Windsor: Windsor Publications (Canada), 1990.

170

_____. *Made in Berlin.* Kitchener: Joseph Schneider Haus Museum, 1989.

Middleton, J.E., and Landon, Fred. *The Province of Ontario—A History, 1615-1927.* 4 vols. Toronto: Dominion Publishing, 1927.

Moyer, Bill. *Kitchener: Yesterday Revisited, an Illustrated History.* Burlington: Windsor Publications (Canada), 1979.

100 Years of Progress in Waterloo County, Canada. Waterloo: The *Chronicle-Telegraph*, 1906.

Peace Souvenir, Activities of Waterloo County in the Great War, 1914-1918. Kitchener: The Kitchener *Daily Telegraph*, 1919.

Public Archives of Canada. Military Records. R.G. 24. H.Q. 593-1-87 (Tappert and Concordia Inquiry) and H.Q. 57-4-77 (Acadian Club Inquiry).

Reaman, G. Elmore. *The Trail of the Black Walnut.* Toronto: McClelland & Stewart, 1957.

Royle, Trevor. *The Kitchener Enigma.* London: Michael Joseph, 1985.

Souvenir of the Golden Jubilee: St. Matthew's Lutheran Church. 1954.

Staebler, Edna. *The Story of Kitchener.* Kitchener: *Kitchener-Waterloo Record*, n.d.

Strack, Johanna Tappert. *Memoirs, Oct. 1892-Nov. 1984.* N.d.

Tappert, Carl Reinhold. *Reminiscences of an Octogenarian.* Philadelphia, 1946.

Tiessen, Paul. *Berlin, Canada: A Self-Portrait of Kitchener, Ontario Before World War One.* St. Jacobs: Sand Hills Books, 1979.

20th Century Souvenir of Busy Berlin: The Best Town in Canada. Berlin: The *News-Record*, 1901.

Warner, Philip. *Kitchener: The Man Behind the Legend.* London: Hamish Hamilton, 1985.

White, Randall. *Ontario, 1610-1915: A Political and Economic History.* Toronto: Dundurn Press, 1985.

Vernon's City of Berlin and Town of Waterloo and Bridgeport Directory. Hamilton, various years.

Winter, Charles F. *Lieutenant-General The Hon. Sir Sam Hughes K.C.B., M.P., Canada's War Minister 1911-1916.* Toronto: Macmillan, 1931.

Wilson, Barbara M., ed. *Ontario and the First World War 1914-1918.* Toronto: University of Toronto Press, 1977.

Uttley, W.V. *A History of Kitchener, Ontario.* Waterloo: Chronicle Press, 1937.

Newspapers

The Berlin *Telegraph*. 1915-17.
The Berlin *News-Record*. 1915-17.
Berliner Journal. 1916.
Guelph Mercury. 1916.
Kitchener-Waterloo Record. 1956, 1966, 1989.
London Advertiser. 1916.
Stratford Herald. 1916.
Toronto Globe. 1916.
Toronto Daily Star. 1916.

Index

173